THE EARLY RECORDS
OF THE
BANKES FAMILY
AT WINSTANLEY

Edited by
JOYCE BANKES
and
ERIC KERRIDGE

MANCHESTER
Printed for the Chetham Society
1973

© 1973 The Chetham Society

Published for the Society by
Manchester University Press
316–324 Oxford Road
Manchester M13 9NR

ISBN 0 7190 1158 2

Printed in Great Britain by Butler & Tanner Ltd., Frome and London

REMAINS

Historical and Literary

CONNECTED WITH THE PALATINE COUNTIES OF

Lancaster and Chester

VOLUME XXI—THIRD SERIES

MANCHESTER:

Printed for the Chetham Society

1973

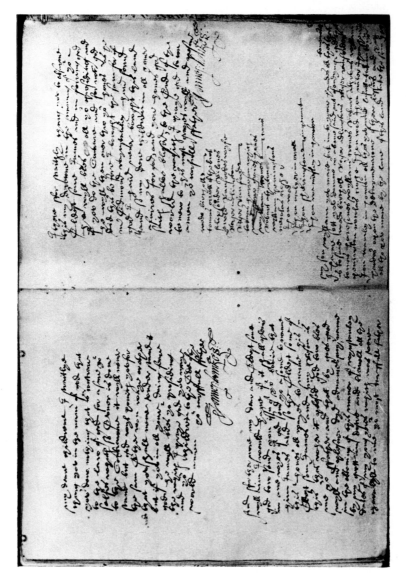

Two pages of the Memoranda Book, bearing signatures of James Bankes. See pp. 33–4, below

CONTENTS

PLATES

MAP

ACKNOWLEDGEMENTS

THE PUBLICATION of this volume has been aided by a generous grant from the British Academy, and Mrs Joyce H. M. Bankes has kindly defrayed the cost of the illustrations. The Council of the Society is grateful for both these subventions.

PREFACE

WINSTANLEY HALL lies in the park of that name about $3\frac{1}{2}$ miles south-west of Wigan. The present building and its tithe barn has been added to at various times during the past 300 years since its Elizabethan origin in the early 1570s. Half a mile away from the present house is a listed homestead moat, possibly the site of the original manor house; three sides of the moat are still visible.

James Bankes (1542–1617), the author of the Memoranda Book which is reproduced here, purchased the Winstanley estate and other surrounding land in 1595/6 from a member of the Winstanley family who would presumably have been responsible for the initial building in stone. The Winstanley property has been in possession of the Bankes family since that time to the present day, and it was early in the 1930s that the Memoranda Book of James Bankes was found among the family papers. Since then it has been used whole or in part on three occasions: (1) it was privately printed for the family in 1935; (2) extracts were used in a paper read to the Lancashire and Cheshire Historic Society in 1942; and (3) as the basis for an article in the *Report* of the Lancashire Record Office in 1961. The current presentation aims at a more detailed analysis with special reference to the agrarian economy of the period.

It has been previously assumed both in the *Victoria County History of Lancashire* and in the 1942 paper that James Bankes was a native of Wigan and that it was from there that he went to London to start his apprenticeship as a goldsmith. While there is much circumstantial evidence for this, there is as yet no concrete proof that this was the case. In the sixteenth century families of that name were established in Westmorland, Craven, the West Riding of Yorkshire, Warwickshire, London, and, 'as tradition reports', in the Isle of Man. The more enterprising of these families made their way south in search of opportunity and advancement. James Bankes was among them. He knew Stowe's London and its merchants, to one of whom he was apprenticed to learn the trade of goldsmith. Others of his name were also in the trade; there is a drinking horn— (*c.* 1500)—with silver gilt mounts in the possession of Christ's Hospital presented by Thomas Bankes in 1602.

James Bankes prospered in his career as goldsmith–banker and invested his money in the northern part of the country, firstly in the manor of Greet in the parish of Yardley near Birmingham, thence to Lancashire where he made several purchases before his acquisition of the manor of Winstanley in the parish of Wigan.

It may be of interest to pick out one or two points from the doctrine

propounded in 1610 and compare these with the farming conditions which
exist at Winstanley today. James Bankes's interest 'as a landlord not only
to farmers but also to coal masters, colliers, millers, cutlers, nailers, and
bowlers' is surely of great importance today. With the end of the coal
mining industry in sight, both in deep and opencast mining, the future
use of the land is one of the very great problems that has to be faced.
Today one has to decide the relative proportions of land to be allocated
to housing, industry, agriculture and forestry, and the ever-growing
problem of providing amenity and recreation for those who live and work
in the district and now have much more leisure than was the case in
James Bankes's day.

A further point is the type of husbandry most suited to the area.
James Bankes had difficulty in deciding the proportion of land which
should be in corn compared to grass. While the introduction of modern
machinery, combine and potato harvesters, has immensely reduced the
labour requirements and cost of arable crops, experience in Winstanley
Park over the past fifteen years has amply demonstrated the advantages of
keeping the corn area to a reasonable proportion of the whole and leaving
the remainder for the feeding of stock.

A final point from the Memoranda Book which may be worth noting
is the paternal counsel given by James to his family in respect of suitable
partners. This guidance in what has been called 'selective marriage' was
a very important feature of the period, whereby financial and territorial
advantages might accrue to the advantage of the main estate. James's heirs
seem to have done their best in this direction; the main line intermarried
with Ireland (Elizabeth, daughter of Sir Thomas Ireland of Bewsey and
a neighbour), later a Royalist from Chastleton House in Oxfordshire, a
Legh of Bruche, Legh of Lyme, a Cholmondeley of Vale Royal in
Cheshire, and in the eighteenth century a Holme of Up Holland, the
latter adding considerably to the territorial holding.

JOYCE BANKES

Winstanley Hall, 1971

INTRODUCTION

IN THE PREFACE an outline has been given of how James Bankes (1542–1617) decided to come to Lancashire and settle at Winstanley near Wigan.[1] Bankes had surely benefited from schooling only to a limited extent. He had been taught something of the then highly-prized three rudiments of learning, and may even have attended a grammar school, but then with meagre success, for a man who had learned some Latin as a lad would hardly have written 'in kapite', 'suchsessor', or 'experiench' (fos. 3r., 25v.). He likely wrote much as he spoke, and then his speech would have been not only in the idiom and accents of his country, but also clumsy and inaccurate, rendering 'purchased' as 'porched' (fo. 3r.), 'persuasions' and 'persuaders' as 'parswagins' and 'parswagyeres' (fo. 10r.) and many other words in an equally misshapen form. The reader will see for himself that spelling and grammar are grievously at fault. Spelling, we know, had not yet been reduced to a single standard, but many of James Bankes's versions failed to conform with any of the usually accepted variations.

These merely scholastic deficiencies, however, in no way prevented him from making his way in the world and turning the stream of his trade into the lake of his country estate. Yet James hardly seems to have been the archetype of the razor-sharp businessman and was perhaps less shrewd than many of his fellows. Cunning rustics like Peter Orrell, John Fairhurst and Robert Atherton, to mention but a few Bankes himself admits to, worsted him shabbily (fos. 5r., 6r., 16v., 17r.). But Bankes had at least one quality that would have stood him in the highest stead in the business he prospered in—his evident probity. He was, it readily appears, an honest, upright, sober, religious man whose word was his bond, trustworthy in dealings and discreet in conversation. His advice was, 'In any company be very silent and use few words' (fo. 9v.), and a man of few words commends himself in transactions where discretion is looked for.

Bankes put a premium on ecclesiastical conformity (fo. 10r.), and was a deeply religious man. He believed in the efficacy of prayer and enjoined it on others (fo. 8r.). True religion was then part and parcel of ordinary life and he thought it nothing strange to call upon or praise God when dealing with everyday affairs. In this he was in step with his fellows and contemporaries, for example, Robert Loder of Harwell.[2] Loder habitually

---

[1] PRO, Du. Lanc. Deps. 55/25; BM, Lans. 56/3, fo. 7v.
[2] *Robert Loder's Farm Accounts 1610–1620* (ed. G. E. Fussell, R. Hist. S., Camd. 3rd. ser., 1936, liii, 10, 34, 36, 37, 38, 48, 53, 60, 62, 79, 81, 86, 96, 101, 106, 109, 110, 118, 122, 124, 129, 131, 140, 143, 146, 147, 161, 162, 165, 168, 173, 177, 181, 183, 184, 185, 189.

praised the Lord for the profits he made by his enterprise, and rightly
felt himself as much at one with God when harvesting as when in church.
No hint of hypocrisy should be seen in this. The fault is not in Loder and
Bankes, but rather in those who regard the lawful quest for profit by
enterprise as irreligious or 'anti-social'. Loder and Bankes understood that
in a free market the man of enterprise earns his profit only by satisfying
the needs and wishes of his fellow men. They rightly assumed, too, that if
each man pursue his own self-interest within the framework of the old
common law, he will at the same time, in the same measure, and by the
self-same deeds, be pursuing the interests of humanity as a whole.

If Bankes showed anything out of the ordinary in his religious feelings,
it was only in a perhaps slightly exaggerated tendency to regard himself
as the avenging angel. He believed not only in doing as one would be
done by, but also in giving no favours to evil-doers. He saw no reason why
he should put himself out for those who had been harsh or deceitful to
himself or to others (fos. 13., 16v., 17, 23v., 24, 28), or why he should
bestow anything upon a man who had 'brought a poor widow into a
miserable estate and want to her utter and great loss and almost undoing'
or taken a tenement over a poor man's head, so that his wife 'died for
very grief' and he himself 'was constrained to make a poor cabin without
the house and enforced to lie upon the ground a whole winter' (fos. 23v.,
24r.). Yet Bankes bore no malice towards a bad and deceitful tenant's
son who was himself as yet an unknown quantity (fo. 14r.). And he dealt
considerately and generously with all his honest tenants. He was, too, a
good friend to the poor (fos. 14, 17r.).

One of James Bankes's most fetching ways was his knowing of himself.
He was a self-made man and proud of it. He had gained Winstanley Hall
by his own efforts, as he said, 'by my great industry and travail all the
days of my young years' (fo. 22v.). Yet he could see himself as others saw
him and realised people might tell his sons, 'Your father was a man
unlearned and God knoweth he did his best, but, alack, he had small skill
in the world' (fo. 9r.).

It might be urged that he prided himself too much upon his achieve-
ments and became a little swollen headed. He displayed a praiseworthy
desire to provide for his own posterity, but seems to have had a sneaking
feeling that posterity's proper function was to reflect glory upon his own
name, especially his own Christian name (fo. 22v.). He showed signs of
doubting, too, quite unfoundedly as it turned out, his offsprings' ability
to do as well as he had done. In his own mind this doubt was inseparable
from his desire to overlook them from the grave. This accounts for the
excessively detailed and tedious advice he pressed on them and for the
earnest and wearisome injunctions to follow it that he never tired of re-
iterating (e.g. fos. 18v., 25). He seems to have expected unswerving com-
pliance with every single one of his instructions, even when these them-

selves countermanded others that had already proved unwise (e.g. fo. 14v.).

At times Bankes appears to overlook the possible benefit to his sons of learning from their own mistakes when doing things for themselves. He almost forgets that it was not long since he had been a tenderfoot on the demesne and a greenhorn in the estate office, and hardly seems to remember the supreme pleasure of finding things out for oneself. Perhaps he still smarted unduly over the remembrance that when first becoming squire in 1595 he was cozened by some of his own tenants (fos. 5r., 6r., 16v., 17r.) and even towards the end of his days he was forced to admit that his agricultural management had resulted in 'loss and undoing' (fo. 25v.).

What he knew about running the estate, he had found out for himself, with little or no professional advice or help. A man in his position, in the lesser or middling gentry, had to act as his own land steward and see to his own estate office as well as manage his own farmland. As he had found things out for himself, nothing could be more natural than that he should believe his discoveries to be unique and imagine himself as blazing a trail for lesser mortals to follow. In sober reality, he had only hit upon what others in his circumstances had known for ages. What was still a cause of wonderment to him was taken for granted in the circles in which they were used to moving. Indeed, everything about Bankes's estate management that was wise was also ordinary and humdrum. This is exactly why his full record of it is so valuable to us. Few or none would have bothered to have set down such commonplaces in black and white. What everyone takes for granted is unlikely to be remarked upon. General assumptions are usually hidden ones. But Bankes artlessly reveals these things to another age, which, in turn, hides its own assumptions in a conspiracy of silence that few will break. Through Bankes's memoranda, then, we can catch a rare glimpse of the realities of life in the Lancashire Plain in the early modern period and gain new insights into landowners and their problems in general.

One of the first things to strike the reader must be that landowners were very far from being merely the owners of land and that even this land was by no means all agricultural. Like most of his kind, our hero was an industrial as well as an agricultural landlord, and a coalowner as well as a landowner. In other words, what we call landowners were owners of land in the most general sense of the totality of natural resources. The land was Bankes's and so was the coal under it and the buildings upon it. He was a landlord not only to farmers, but also to coalmasters and colliers, millers, cutlers, nailers and bowlers. His interests, therefore, were in promoting mines, mills and manufactures as well as agriculture (fos. 4v., 12v., 13v., 17v.–19, 25r., 27v., 30v. and 1667 rental). His grandson derived about £100 a year from coalmines.[1] Thus, to identify the landowners' with the

---

[1] Lancs. Rec. Off. DDBa, Colliery accounts, 1676–96. J. Bankes, 'Recs. of Mining in Winstanley and Orrell', *Trans. Lancs. and Ches. Antig. Soc.*, 1939, liv, 44.

agricultural interest, as many have done, is wholly fallacious, and to suppose that landowners generally favoured agricultural interests against industrial ones is folly mounted upon stilts. Yet how often do we still read of the landowners' antagonism to industry, of their enacting of the Corn Laws out of regard to their own selfish interests, and such like? The truth rather is, that since landowners stood to gain from all sorts and kinds of economic progress and from all branches of human industry, they were truly the residual beneficiaries of everyone else and so represented all their interests. It goes without saying that when changes were required in the interests of all, some landowners were by nature more intelligent and far-sighted than others, and that some of them advocated measures that others had not yet come to accept. The simple truth is that human beings of all kinds and conditions act according to their varying degrees of understanding and reason.

The second strikingly obvious fact the reader may discover for himself from Bankes's memoranda is the utter unreality of the views, so constantly and strenuously put forward by some socialists, that early modern English landowners flourished by rack-renting and otherwise oppressing their poor tenants. Fortunately, James Bankes thought it necessary to explain, at least to himself, the common policy of landowners, which was to let their tenants sit at easy rents on long leases of three lives or twenty-one years, and so to encourage them to improve their farms and offer competitive entry fines. In this way the landowner was above any reproach of dealing unkindly or unlovingly with his tenants, seeing that he took nothing but was freely proffered and esteemed reasonable by all, and yet maximised his own income while assuring the maintenance and accumulation of capital, and so automatically enhancing the well-being of consumers in general[1] (fos. 8v., 9r., 12r., 15, 17v.). The interests of landlord and tenant needed no reconciliation; they coincided of their own accord. Each followed his own interests and so directly benefited each other, and indirectly the worker and consumer. This is why we read nothing of landlords grinding the faces of the poor, and much of some tenants oppressing their own kind (fos. 5r., 6r., 16v., 17). Truly, a few of them were not a little cruel to their fellows.

To be or become a landowner was to prefer some future to some present income, not merely for oneself alone, or for one's children as well, but also for one's children's children, and for countless generations to come. Having made a fortune, one might spend it on oneself or one's own, or speculate further with it, or secure it in land, where it would endure as capital for many generations and not a few centuries, provided only that it was looked after, maintained and preserved, and not consumed. Careful provision for the future was thus the hallmark of the

[1] See 'The Movement of Rent, 1540–1640', in *Essays in Economic History* (ed. E. M. Carus-Wilson), vol. ii, London, 1962, pp. 208 *sqq.*

rising or firmly established landed gentleman as opposed to the improvidence of the falling. All one had to do to decline from the ranks of the landed gentry was to prefer present to future satisfaction to a degree that entailed the consumption of capital. Edmund Winstanley appears to have been the victim less of the economic circumstances of his time than of his own actions in the face of them. James Bankes says as much when he remarks, 'If Mr Edmund Winstanley had served God, I had never bought his land' (fo. 23r.). Even before this, it should be noted, Winstanley had been reduced to the shift of disposing of various parts of the demesne lands there.[1]

Consequently, having bought the estate, Bankes was confronted with the task of restoring these alienated parts. At the same time he was concerned to achieve the best possible disposition as between the hall and the tenant farms. We see him adding to the demesne in some places, selling off remote parts of the estate elsewhere, notably the portion of the manor of Winstanley that lay detached at Whiston, and sometimes dividing up tenements to get a better return from them. But were any tenant displaced by these rearrangements, Bankes spared no pains to find him another and equivalent farm (fos. 10v., 12v., 15r., 18, 20r., 27v., 28). He was greatly concerned, too, to improve the present and future value of Winstanley as a gentleman's residential estate by ridding the demesne of the unsightly cottages the Winstanleys had allowed to be built within the ring fence and in full view from the Hall. James makes no bones about advising his heirs to pull these down and sell off the timber and other material from them (fos. 14, 18, 19r., 28). This may strike some readers as harsh, but let it be noted that Bankes dispossessed no one, invoked no compulsory purchase order, forced no sale at a derisory price, and sequestrated nothing belonging to others. He simply waited for the leases to expire and then did as he listed with his own, which is the right of every freeborn Englishman. So far from being a hard landlord, he was a good friend to his tenants and succoured the widows and orphans (fos. 12v., 14r., 17r., 24v., 28v.).

Exactly how much improvement James Bankes was able to make in his lands and rents and fines, we cannot say. We only can see that the value of his estate was rising in his own lifetime. As time went by he frequently raised his estimates of the yearly values of various of the holdings (e.g. fo. 16v.). Precious as his memoranda are, one cannot help reflecting how much more valuable they would have been for students like us had the doubtlessly

[1] Edm. Winstanley, s. of Th. W. by his w. Eliz., d. of Sir Gilbert Gerard; after his f.'s death 1561 his m. married Jn Bradshaw of Presteigne, Rads.. Edm. also intermarried with the B. family. His only s. Chas died 1578 & was buried at P.. Edm. was sheriff for Pembs. 1590 & for Rads. 1592–3 & 1599–1600. He died as 'of St Dogmaels Abbey Radnor' 1612, leaving no male issue. J. B.'s censure may have referred to absentee land-ownership in general rather than to any specific misdemeanour on the part of E. W.. To J. B. this desertion of one's patrimony must have seemed hard to understand or forgive.

no less interesting book of account he mentions (fo. 25v.) not been lost, mislaid or destroyed. With these two together, much greater construction could have been put upon each, and we could have discovered far more about the cultivation of the demesne and the management of the estate than we can now hope to know.

Nevertheless, what little we know of Bankes's running of the demesne, is highly instructive. He paid close attention to matters of husbandry, as well he might, for it brought him in not much less than his lettings. As was his wont, he found things out for himself, and discovered what was already the usual and best plan of management throughout his own country. Once again what he has to say is noteworthy not for its originality, for this was conspicuous only by its absence, but on account of its eventual conformity with the standard and long-established practice of his neighbours and peers in the Lancashire Plain.[1] It was, with minor exceptions, a country of enclosed fields, which were mostly employed in up-and-down husbandry. The greensward was inverted for a crop of oats, usually followed by barley, and then perhaps by oats again. These two were the chief crops, and the lesser ones wheat, peas, beans and buckwheat ('French wheat'). Two, three or four such crops were taken before the land was laid down again to about seven years of grass. This is exactly what the reader will find in Winstanley demesnes if he works out the rotations in particular fields as recorded in the accounts appended herein and on folio 16v. of the memoranda. Most of the land was arable, but under this system at least half, usually more, of the arable was in grass. Moreover, some permanent grassland was also to be found, so that all told only modest proportions of the whole were tilled at any one time. The Bankes family, including James in his last and better informed years, normally ploughed about twenty acres a year. Barley and oats were both malted, but the best or 'Eastern' malt had to be purchased from the more favoured cereal countries of England, such as the Midland Plain, through markets like Chester, Halifax, Liverpool and Derby. (Incidentally, gentlemen, farmers and others brewed their own ale and beer, and it is interesting to see the same custom of brewing special March beer in this country in the seventeenth century as in Bavaria in the twentieth.) Sheep were stocked far less than cattle. James had fewer of them even in summer, when it was usual to buy in extra drafts; and in value they stood in the ratio of one to ten. Horse teams, or mixed ones of oxen led by horses, were usually employed. A few cow beasts were fattened on grass or in their stalls on hay, corn and pulse; but the grand objective in farming was the rearing of cattle bought as young stores from the North Country (fo. 22 and inventory).

All this, and no doubt much more, Bankes stumbled upon himself after much trial and error. At first he jumped to the conclusion that tillage was the husbandman's highest profit-maker, which in the Lancashire Plain it

[1] E. Kerridge, *The Agricultural Revolution*, London (Allen & Unwin), 1967, pp. 144-6.

certainly was not; and, judging by the sharp way in which he condemns the practice, he may well have at one time tried breeding his own cattle, which would have been a serious error (fo. 22), but one he had probably corrected, or decided to correct, by the time of his death, when he left only eight calves. (His seventeen cows were not necessarily or probably all female, for 'cow' was even then a generic term as in 'cow-town', 'cow-boy' etc.) It would have been strange indeed if his attention had not been attracted to marling, for the farmers of the Lancashire Plain made a great virtue of it;[1] and he seems to have unearthed the truism that marl improved crops and raised rents (fos. 10v., 15, 16r.). Yet it was some time, perhaps, before he realised that continual marling of the same field eventually led to the saturation of the land and sharply diminishing returns. Thus he first advises his son to be 'a continual marler of your demesne', whereas it was only much later he felt constrained to add the postscript, 'Marl that which was never afore marled, and no more meddle not withall in any wise, the charge is great therein' (fo. 15r.). He revealingly failed to add that this charge, if in marling too long or too often, was also a positive misinvestment, and he fell far short of indicating the correct policy to adopt when marling showed diminishing returns, namely, to lime the marled ground.

The reason Bankes stated for finally and tardily deciding that it was best to grow no more corn than to supply the consumption of hall, house and farm was, rather strangely, not that it was better for more corn to be bought from another country where cereal-growing was more productive, which was obvious to most farmers in the Lancashire Plain, but the great charges he had been at in keeping servants in husbandry, to his 'loss and undoing'. But this should be taken as an indirect way of saying that the costs of corn-growing were too high in the Lancashire Plain and that the comparative advantage lay elsewhere. 'I have', he writes, 'been hindered by keeping of servants in getting of corn, so that I have rather desired to die than to live, for they care not whether end goeth forward, so that they have meat, drink and wages. Small fear of God is in servants.' (fo. 25v.) Since this opinion was evidently formed in or shortly before 1610, it is doubly significant, being, as it is, more or less contemporaneous with Robert Loder's judgments that 'all workmen almost ... will play legerdemain with their masters and favour themselves', that 'men can work if they list and so they can loiter', and that his stole £2 worth of corn from him a year. By 1613 he, too, was confronted by forbidding wage-costs and resolved to economise on wage-labour as far as possible.[2] This coincidence seems to point to a period of acute labour shortage and its natural accompaniment of unruly labourers between about 1608 and 1619. That labour-costs should have worried Loder at this time is perfectly

[1] *Ibid.* 246–8.
[2] *Robert Loder's Farm Accounts*, pp. 25, 56, 59, 72, 90, 122.

understandable. He was, after all, first and foremost a corn-grower. Indeed, the comparative advantages of the Lancashire Plain and the Chalk
Country are no way more clearly shown than in the fact that Bankes
curtailed cereal production and Loder did not. It is all the more remarkable
that Bankes should have had the same labour problem as Loder. Indeed,
it is only comprehensible by reference to the fact, to which he himself
confessed, that he had been tilling far too much land. Once the dangerous
policy of farming the Lancashire Plain as though it were the Chalk Country had been abandoned, the labour problem must have loomed less large.
In 1674–5, for instance, when the tillage in Winstanley demesne amounted
to about 18½ acres, most of the labour would have been supplied by the
tenants' rent services, which included 3¾ acres ploughing, 10 days ploughing, and harrowing, shearing, mucking out and muck-spreading to match.

As we have seen, James Bankes, as we all do, lived and learned. He
enjoyed the Winstanley estate long enough to see his own fallibility and
change his own mind. There is, indeed, no tutor to match experience.
Thus we find him at first sternly advising his heirs as follows: 'I would
have you to make as much tillage as possibly you always can and to get
corn, for therein is the most profit of husbandry, for in breeding of cattle
is great loss, and make tillage of your best land that is good and therein
your gain will be greatest, for corn is ready money and cometh once a year.'
(fo. 22r.) Later he entirely altered his mind and delivered it in the following terms: 'Since, my son, that I did set down here in this book my
opinion for the good of thee and thy posterity, I have further made
consideration for the benefit of thee and those that shall come after thee
and have found the same most for your good by common experience and
most sound proof to my great hindrance and loss as appeareth by my
book of account plainly to be seen from year to year as followeth the great
charges that I have been at in keeping servants to do my husbandry to
my loss and undoing. Therefore, my son, in the name of God, follow my
counsel herein. Make no more tillage to get corn than to serve your house'.
(fo. 25v.) This parallels his earlier advocacy of liberal, almost unlimited,
marling and his later policy of restriction. Similarly with estate management, at first he wanted certain cottages pulled down, and then later
ordered them to be reserved for the use of colliers (fos. 18, 19v.). Earlier
on, too, he puts his trust in low rents and high fines, promising at least
£80 a year in fines over and above the ancient rents (fo. 12r.). Afterwards,
in 1610, he countermands this and charges his son to let many tenements
as annual tenancies at rack rents (fos. 13, 14v., 17v., 18, 19v., 24v.). 'My son',
he says, 'where I have advised thee to make leases when any tenement
shall fall, I have found it by common experience greatly to the contrary,
therefore . . . when any lease shall fall to thee, let the same to the tenant
again for a yearly rent, and in God's name take not too much rent nor yet
too little, for a mean is the best, so shalt thou be best able to live.' (fo. 26r.)

PLATE ONE   Two pages of the Memoranda Book. See pp. 20–1, below

These changes of course, it may well be argued, were due less to the correction of mistakes than to adjustment to altered circumstances. If, as apparently he did, Bankes had formerly marled liberally, this would explain why he later revised his views. Indeed, there is every reason to suppose that Winstanley was no exception to the general rule that marling reached saturation point in much of the land of the Lancashire Plain, though not, of course, in newly-drained mosses, somewhere about the end of the sixteenth century.[1] This would also go a long way to explain why James ceased to regard tillage as a great source of profit, since it was only for a limited time after marling that long successions of tillage crops were practicable. The tightness of the labour market was undoubtedly another consideration. And since marling was the chief improvement open to farmers in the Lancashire Plain at that time, and apparently the only one that Bankes gave much weight to, and since long leases with low rents and high entry fines were essentially improving leases, that is, were the ones that enabled farmers to profit themselves while advantaging their land-lords, once this marling became less frequently an eligible improvement or perhaps even a waste of money, no reason for improving leases might be thought any longer to have existed, and annual tenancies with rack rents would then be best adapted to the new situation where improvements were hardly to be expected and price and rent falls to be feared. We have no reason, then, lightly to assume that Bankes's changes of mind were due altogether to the correction of error, or that he was necessarily any less right in his first set of advice than in his second and contradictory one.

That even the best-laid plans are apt to go awry, though it may not have been brought home quite so forcibly then as now, was nevertheless part of the common stock of human wisdom in those days. Even if all James Bankes's business decisions had been justified by later events the great fault to be found with his testament to his children is precisely his failure to recognise that set plans for an uncertain future make no sense and that it is useless to lay down detailed instructions for posterity. Bankes was succeeded by his son William (1593–1666) and he in turn by another William (1631–76). What William the elder thought of these two con-tradictory sets of hard and fast instructions is neither recorded nor difficult to guess. He could have been forgiven for thinking his father's anxious solicitude exaggerated and his judgment fallible. After all, there was no more reason to suppose circumstances would be less changeable after than before James's death. He had the choice of faithfully following his father's instructions in detail on all points and so gradually losing the estate he had built up or of ignoring them in favour of acting as his father would have done under similar circumstances and so being faithful to his memory and life's work.

[1] Kerridge, *Agricultural Revolution*, p. 248.

This prompts us to ask whether or not the two Williams followed
James's instructions, a question that can be addressed only to the rentals
and accounts made in and after the time of the second William. These
were records made in the ordinary course of business by the steward
employed by the family. They have been included here less for their
intrinsic interest than for collation with the Memoranda Book and the
inventory. The steward, of course, was not concerned to show anything
in the nature of a profit-and-loss account, but merely to quit himself of
what was charged to him in the course of his managerial duties, which
consisted of collecting rents, mill-tolls and impropriated tithes, supplying
grain and other produce for the hall, by purchase if need be, and disposing
of it as required, to the chief servant in husbandry for seed-corn and stock-
feed, and to the stable-boy for the riding horses. The early accounts were
more summary, but after 1673 they include daily entries of receipts and
disposals at the granary. All the accounts are made up in an orderly
fashion in a ledger, and they maintain the same high standard almost to
the end. The rentals are entered in the same ledger turned upside down
and used in reverse. The early ones are undated, but apparently belong to
the mid 1660s. In 1669 a much fuller rental, including the boon and labour
rents, was made out; but afterwards followed a reversion to the practice
of merely summarising the money rents. Otherwise these documents call
for little remark. They are wholly conventional and valuable to us mainly
for the light they shed on estate management after James's death.

The two Williams certainly proved themselves no worse landlords than
James had been. Rents were remitted to poor widows and other needy
souls. But nothing indicates that annual tenancies were generally adopted.
On the contrary, the ancient rents continued much as before. On the
other hand, the cottages within the ring yard had all disappeared by
1770 at the latest, as the map made in that year clearly shows,[1] and as
far as can be seen few or none survived in 1669, although from a mere
rental it is admittedly difficult to distinguish an old cottage from a new
grant in lieu. As for tillage, it is abundantly clear that the second William
restricted it to the purposes of his own domestic and farm consumption.
An occasional surplus for sale seems to have been the purely accidental
result of an unforeseen and extraordinarily high yield. The accounts show
little evidence of marling, and then only on a small scale under except-
tional circumstances, and the yields of corn in terms of the ratio of harvest
to seed, as far as they can be made out, appear to demonstrate at one
and the same time both why it was unprofitable to grow much corn and
that little or no new marling was undertaken. In short, William's policy
was sometimes in accord with his grandfather's advice in its latest form,
sometimes not.

[1] Lancs. Rec. Off., DDBa, Map of the lands belonging to Wm Bankes Esq. lying in
Winstanley and some little in Orrel, 1770.

In so far as his successors practised what James preached this by no means proves they followed his advice. Inasmuch as he only enjoined on them what was the normal, everyday practice of landowners and cultivators in the Lancashire Plain, it would be just as logical to suppose his heirs simply followed not his suit but theirs, and it would be gratuitous to assume they learned the facts of life from his lips alone. If a man advise his sons to do as others do, and they do so, this proves nothing as to the heeding of the advice, for most persons do as others, whether so advised or not. Moreover, experience tends to show that sons pay less attention to their parents' precepts than to their practices. When the same policies were continued, it could have been from mere force of inertia. Furthermore, great minds think alike, and if the father thought the cottages in the ring yard an eyesore, so probably would ninety-nine persons out of a hundred.

Only one piece of paternal advice stands out as a distinctly novel and individual opinion, and that is the proposal to switch to annual tenancies at rack rents. If either William had meant to follow this advice to the letter, he would have made this change. But this is the one injunction they showed least sign of obeying. Why, we cannot be sure. They may have considered the idea and rejected it, or they may not have given it another thought. If they had consciously rejected this counsel, they would have had good grounds for so doing, for in fact all the steam had not yet gone out of improvement in the Lancashire Plain by 1610, for liming still remained, and further opportunities for drainage, which entailed initial marling. Room could almost certainly be found for improving leases in Winstanley as elsewhere. But let us not speculate too much about these matters. All the history of ideas is bedevilled by the sparsity of evidence of the transmission of ideas and thoughts, and this simple case is no exception to the general rule.

In fine, the moral seems to be that the world is to be ruled from neither the cradle nor the grave.

* * * * *

James Bankes's Memoranda Book hereinafter transcribed is upon paper with a BO urn watermark, $10\frac{1}{5} \times 7\frac{3}{10}$ inches to a page, bound in leather with a clasp, and in fair condition. The main part is apparently in his hand, but the many addenda are mostly in another, rather better formed, possibly that of his wife or one of his sons. These addenda are in italics in the ensuing text, and the marginalia of them are also indented. A few eighteenth-century insertions are merely by way of defacement and have been ignored. The accounts and rentals appended were made on paper $5\frac{4}{5} \times 14\frac{1}{5}$ inches to the page, watermarked CAB, bound and well preserved. James's will was proved in the Consistory Court of Chester and both it and the inventory reprinted here are now deposited in the Lancashire Record Office.

The two editors bear joint responsibility for the Memoranda Book. The second named of them has dealt with the Inventory, the Rentals and the Accounts and has compiled the indices.

E. K.

THE MEMORANDA BOOK
OF JAMES BANKES

[On flyleaf at beginning]

x*li.*   Delevered to my wyf to kepe laist of November 1610 the sum of tene pondes in a bleder.

lx*li.*   Ther is more under my bed thre skower pondes in a hoies of kerse.

xi*li.*   Ther is more in my chist in the conteng houes alevene pondes. Resarvid all this money again tow the biing of land.

[fo. *3r*]

THE Eyght daye of October in the xxviii yeare of quene Elezabeath, I James Bankes dyd bye of Alyxandor Avenone of London marchant the maner of Grett[1] lying in Wostershere wythin parrish of Yardley, as apereth by the said evedences maid from the said Alixonder unto the same James Bankes for ever, wyth all such other assurances as therunto belongeth, the which landes was porched by Sir Alixander Avenon father of the said Alixonder the sone and are to Sir Alixonder whom was lord mare of the sete of London whom porched the said maner of kyng Henre the Eyght upon the sobepression of the abbes and so by which

760. 0. 0   mene the landes are houlden in kapete of the quene and her suchsessor, wheareof theare is yearely to be payd owt the tenement of the ould rent which is about xxii*s.* as I take it, the which rent is payd by the tenant that hath the leais maid by Sir Alexonder Avenone whom porchesed the same of the kyng in a bok and so possessed it from the kyng in a bok of an Mr Throgmorten whom maid an asinement therof out of his said boke to Sir Alixander Avernon and his ares for ever as the comen youes is in such lyke porchesing of the kyng or the quene maid upon such grett sales. The leas was mayd for fyfte yeares by Sir Alixander Avenon and at such tymes as I porchesed the sam ther was to com unspent in the leas abowt xxiii yers and the rent therof is to be payd at the fest of Sint Mycholl Earkangell and on Ladie daye in Lent or wythin forte dayes after, ten pond at a pament; the sam is to be payd at the fount stone in Powles church[2] and

---

[1] Greet, 1½ m. S.S.E. of Birmingham.   [2] St Paul's, London.

for non pament therof to forfet at evere tym fyfe pondes and so to destraine for the rent and the forfetoure for so it is mayd in the les and forthermor ther is to be payd by the lord into Mr Osbornes offis in the Checker for a respytt of omyg evere fyft terme vj*s*. iiii*d*. [fo. 3*v*.] And upon evere such pament you shall resave aqutances for the sam. But in ane wyes se that you paye this vi*s*. iiii*d*. evere fyfe tearme or other wyes ther wyl be sent fourth of the Exchekker prosis for the same and so fined evere term thell the sam be payd, for so I have bene sarvid myself in this behalfe. You shall fynd all the evedences of this land in a whitt wodden boix inclosed in a whitt lether baig seled up rond abowt the sell and allso opon the baig you shall find wrytt wyth myne one hand thes wordes, that is to saye, inclosed is the evedences of the maner of Gritt in Wostershere which cost me in rede money seven hondreth and thre skoure pondes for the which all prase honer and glorie be geven to God amene.

I have sould this said maner to on Henre Gresould who was tenant to the sam and I have him and on other bond wyth him in recognisances to paye six hondreth pondes by a hondreth pond a yere in grees in hole on the second daye of November all wayes [fo. 4*r*.]

The one and twente daye of Januare in the eygt and thirtee yeare of ower soferant lade quene Elezabeth, I James Bankes dyd bye of Edmond Wynstanneley of Prestene[1] in Radnor-sher in Wales the manor of Wynstanley lying in the parrish of Wegan wythin the conte of Lankester, for the which said maner ther was payd in rede money wythin the spaces of tow yeres the som of thre thousand and won hondreth pondes, as apereth by the evedences of the said porchas the which by Good helpe you shall fynd in my conteng houes in chist wyth a nomber of owld rityng and evedences toching the said maner and ollso you shall fynd a fine and a recovere wyth the said evedences from Mr Edmonde Wynstannely oll of them together in a blak boix covered wyth lether and seled up together, for the which I most homly praies my God for the sam and for oll his manefowld blessing bestoid opon me.

3,100*li*.

Amen.
[fo. 4*v*.]

The ninthe day of Aprell in the eyght and thritete yere of ower soferant lade quene Elyzabeth, I James Bankes dyd bye of Rechard Orell and Peter Orrell one tenement wyth 2

----

[1] Presteigne.

or thre cotagus lying in Orrell as apereth by the evedences, of
the anchant rent of twente and 8 sheleng or there abott,
290. 0. 0.   for the which I payd the som of tow hondreth fore skower
and tene ponds. *There is good stor of coles therin praies God for
the sam.* And the tow coteges the rent of them is 2s. apies
1. 1. 8   which is in all wyth the tenement about thrte and on
sheleng and 8d.

[fo. 5r.]

The nint daye of Aprell in the eight and thittert yeare of
quene Elezabeath I maid a leas to Peter Orrell of a houes in
Pemarton wheropon the said Peter Orrell payd for the
same in biing a tenement in Orrell of him wyth 2 cotages
belongeng therunto abowt the som of on hondreth and
fifte pondes and of fines the sam leais *maid* I paissed a fine
to Rauefe Worley of Pemarton to the uces of Francys
Sherington dowring the conteneuanes of the said leais for
the said thre lyfes therin contened. And you shall fynd
the said conterpane of the said fine so passed wythin the
boix wher the evedences of the said laind is oll together,
and therfor my child if it shall plaies God ever to send the said
hous to ane of you depart no more wyth the sam, for I
bought a tenement of the said Peter Orrell and he desavid
me therin att the lest 4 hondreth marks by a cosning
devices alegeng ther was grett store of coles therin and so I
passed my houes in Pemarton for nothing.

[fo. 6r.]

The 8the daye of Julye 1598 I bowght of Denies Hartrig
of Essix all his intrest that he haid in sevene howsus standyng
in Long Lane aturning to Smyth Fild at London the which
he haid by the marrig of Sara Sherrington dowter of
Wyllam Sherrington by a les for a thousand yeares mayd
to the said Wyllam Sherington by on Castell oner of the said
lands and the said les so bowight of Denes Hartrig I only
bowght the sam to my second child Thomas Bankes and for
his only proferment to manten him to larning and therfor
in the name of God lett no man hender him of the sam after
my deses for my trust is in God that he wylbe an aid to the
rest of his brothers if God bles him wyth lyfe and after the
deses of Mr Denies Hartrig then my son is bot to injoye the
on half and during the said les for a tousand yeares, which
grand les remaneth in the handes of Mr Denies Hartrig by
reson ther is eyght housus leing in the sam land mor of the
said landes as I tak if of the rent of 37–6–8, and you shall
find the conveances in my evedences maid from Den

Hartrig to my son, to Master Bankes the yearly rent is 24–13–4, and after the deses of Den Hartrig then my son is to have but the on half and his cossins Mr Jhon Andrus sones the other half, for so it was geven by ther ant Sara Sherrington wyf to Den Hartrig.

[fo. 6v.]

The first daie of October in the second yeare of king James dyd I bye of Tomas Southworth and Jhon Sothworth his son and aire a small towone or hamlett caled by the nam of Howton[1] lying neare unto the towne of Wynwyke[2] of the anchent rent of fiftene pondes and od money, for the which I paid for the sam the som of seven hondreth and xx*li*. besides all other chag that the said Mr Sotthworth dyd powt me untow after that I haid bougt the sam land most wrongfully at the lest forte ponds so the sam standeth me in 700. This land cost me at the fyrst and last vii hondreth and xx *li*. oll in rede money besides all my chards the which I was putt untow by Mr Tomas Sothworth.

720–0

li.

–720–

James Bankes

The fortene daie of June 1611 James Banks of Wynstanley did bye of Mr James Wynstanley of the Blakle Horst fyfe tenements as apereth by the indenture of bargan and saele from the said James Wynstanley and for the which said fyfe tenements the said James Bankes paid for the same the som of fyfe hondreth and 18 *li*. six shelengs and 8*d*. besides the charg of the fine which cost 7*li*. besides my charges tow London which cost tene pondes.

li. s. d.
518. 6. 8

[fo. 8r.]

In the most holye and reverent name of God my deare and swyitt savoire Jhesus Christ harkene and gyve eire my deare cheldren to youre most carfull Fathers advices, the which by Goodes helpe is the vere rode waye to eternall lyfe, for ower savoire Christ saith first seke the kyndom of hevan and oll thing shall be geven unto you, and therefor my deare cheldren in Goodes most holye and reverent nam folow this my derecone. Fyrst evere night whene you go to bed cowle together youer famelye and sarve God acordyng to the boke of comen praier for the daye that past is most homly opon youer knies desiring the Lord to bles you that

[1] Houghton.   [2] Winwick ,3 m. N. of Warrington.

night and for evermore. Amen. And so my deare children in Goods most holye name evere morning whene you ries sarve God privilye in your closett or chamber befor you have any conferences wyth any man whattsoever, youreself alone, and give the only Lord of hevene oll praies and thankes for oll his blesing bestoid opon you. Amen.

And so desiring God to gid you that daye foloing wyth his most holy speritt wyth wysdom and wytt to gid and governe youerselfes in such order and sort as it maye ples God and the world and in thus doing my deare children ther is now dout but that the Lord God of hevene wyll bowth bles youe and youres. Amen. I praye God.

[fo. 8v.]

My deare children unto whom it shall pleas God to injoye this power houes of Wynstanley, I would advices you in Good most holye nam that you wold not in ane wyse deale harlye wyth ane tenant otherwyse then in this order and sort, that is to saye, I would have evere man to injoye his tenement dowring his les and his wyfes lyfe so after to his son if he have ane, and the les being ended I would have you, becaues your rentes is small and not sofesaint to mantene yor home and fammele, to lett his son that is next unto it to make him a les of the said farme in this order and sort as herafter foloith, that is to saie, if the farme be worth twente ponds a yeare, as ther is som, I wold have you to take but sixtene *li.* a yeare rent and so to mak him a les ether son or dowter that was borne upon the sam farme, paying sixtene pondes a yeare for rent for the sam which is worth twente pondes a yeare and lykwyes if a farm shall fawle to you worth sixtene pondes a yeare I wold have you to tak twenty markes a yeare and to mak him lykwyes a les of the sam farm as above ether son or dowter, and so if a farm shall fall that is worth twente markes a yeare then I wold have you to tak tene pondes a yeare and [fo. 9r.] so if a farm shall fawle that is worth tene pondes ayear I wold have you to tak 8*li.*a yeare rent and so tow full forte sheleng or thrte or twente or tene onder the walow or worth therof of the said farmes in the nam of God, and to be vere kynd and loving unto youre tenantes and so they wyll love you in good and godly sort, the which I praye God long to contenew to his most gloreoues wyll and plesure, and in obsarving this order and rulle bowth you and youer houes shall lyve in worship and credit to the glory of God and the joye and comford of yor wyfes and cheldren from aige to aig, to Goods good

plesure and therfor my deare children in the nam of the
moist loving God parforme and kype this rowle and order
that there I have sett you done in Good most holy nam.
And if it shall fawle owt that ane man shall parswaid you
to olter or chang this my derecone in the name of God
asent not unto them for I warrent you that you shall have
grett parswagins to olter and chang the sam and shall sa
yor father was a man unlerned and God knoweth he dyd
his best but alak he haid small skill in the world and therfor
I would tak the advices of such won or of such a on whom is
bowth wyes and larned and I warrant you he will geve you
good consell fitt to sarfe yor terme.

[fo. 9v.]

But my dear and loving children, if you folowe ane other
consell then this that I wyth grett care I have sett you done
bouth you and youre postarete shal be in grett danger to
decaye yor estaitt, but if you folow my consell and derecone
bowthe you and youre houes wyll stand and increais wyth
worshipe and lyving and therfor my deare and loving
childrene let not ane man or woman parswaid you to the
contrare and so in the most holy nam of Jhesus Christ keipe
thes my derecone and in oll yor afares feare God and obey
yor princes wyth oll dewtefulness. Amene.

I praye God even to the end of the world that you and
yor posterete maye feare him, so shall you be sure of eternell
lyfe and yor houes to contenew wyth worshipe and creditt
to Goods good pleasure and to the joye of all youre frends.
Amen.

And forthermore my deare children in all plasus where
you shall com in ane compene be vere silent and youes few
wordes so shall you ples God and the world best and so lest
ofend ane man, and therfor in Good most holye nam never
asent tow olter or chang this my derecone that I have here
set you done 1598 and lett my advices be axsetabyll unto
you my deare children in Gods most holye name so be it,
I most homlye bege the same at the hands of God. Amen.

James Bankes

[fo. 10r.]

My vere deare and loving children, in Good most holye
nam, I would advices you to take this my consell that whene
it shall pleaies God to inabyll you wyth sofecant yeares of
decrecone and strainke of bodye and also sofesant of abelete
to manetene your estaitt that then I would advices you in the
most holye feare of God to make your choies of such wyefes

that fereth God and are obedeant to the princes laies and of
good parantaige borne, for so shall you therby be strenkened
wyth frendes,[1] and seke to mach youreselfes wyth dowters
and ares as neare as you can, for so by the helpe of God is
the sonist waye to increais yor howsus, as mane wyes men
have done hertofore, the which I cowld laye yow done by
partecolarate and therfor my deare and most loving childrene,
folow this my advices and consell in whatsoever I shall
advices you herunto. Lett not ane fine wytt parsaid you to
the controre, for mane parswagyeres shall be to advies you
som on waye and som another, but in Good most holye nam
folo non but myne only, lett all sa what the wyll ane waye
the can.

[fo. 10v.]

My deare child unto whom it shall pleais God to injoye
this powere houes of Wynstarnleye, I would advices you
that wheare there is morerich grond that *when ane shall
fawele unto you*[2] that you would marle the said morich ground,
for ther is marell good store tord the forther sid of the sam
for so was my intendment and after the sam so marled you
maye lett the sam for a marke a naker at the lest and the
charg of the marlyng of an acare wyll stand you in fyfe
markes so that therby you shall incres yor rentes in good
sort wyth Gods helpe and so profare yor tenantes if you
desire not the sam yorselfes, the which I think is not best,
and besides ther is a tenement coled Wyllam Bartons of the
Brone Heth that conteneth abowt sixten acares or thera-
bowts wherin is vere good marrell and if the sam shall fall
to you by ane good sort lykwyes marrell the sam, for the
rent is small at such tymes as I porchesed the sam, but if the
sam tenement be well lok into and marreld it wyll yeald
yow at the lest *fyfe*[3] pondes a yeare rent and therfor my
deare child tak this my consel and be not parsweded to the
contrare.

*And so marlell the sam and after lett the sam for a good rent as you
well maye if the sam shall fall to you or if you can by in the leais
and use it in this sort as I have advised you for the incresing of
yor rent.*

[fo. 11r.]

Besides my deare children ther is a farme wherein on

---

[1] Here are struck out the words 'wyth which at end the Lord shall laye upon you and
youre wyves my deare children'.
[2] Here are struck out the words 'a parsell of the demane'.
[3] 'ten' struck out.

Necolas Crosse dwelleth and haith no child so that the
farme wyll fall in short time to you and hender no man as
apereth by the conterpane of the said les, the which I would
have you to marrell the sam or eles to lett the sam to som at
a resonabyll rent, for I think you maye lett the sam for the
yearelye rent of fower pondes a yeare if so be that you
thinke it good. And forthermore opon the death of the said
Necoles you are to paye unto his wyfe the som of fyfe pondes
wythin forte dayes or eles the sam les conteneweth for the
tearme of tow lyfes more as apereth by the conterpane of the
said les, the which you shall find among the conterpanes of
oll the lessus I have in my costode, and therfor in the nam of
God se the said fyfe pondes be payd acordynglye, otherwyes
you shall be grettly be damnefid of yor leving.

Ther was a les maid to Jhon Wod by Mr Edmond Wynstanley, of whome I bowg this land, of a parsell of grondes
colled the Har Houes Ground which ollwayes belonged to
the manteneances of the hole of Wynstanley, and the said
grond colled the Har Houes Grond being morged by Mr
Edmond Wynstanley to the said John Woid and so forfeted
dyd take the benefitt therof contrare to all *uncharetabyll*
delyng and at such tymes as Mr Wynstanley maid the saill
to me the said Bankes then the said Bankes dyd bye all

[fo. 11v.] posibyll menes intrett the said Jhon Wod to take his money,
but by no meanes he would dow, so the best end that I
Bankes cowld bring him untow was *to confirm his*[1] les and in
consetheracone therof the said John Wod did lend me the
said Bankes a hondreth pond for a yeare and this was the
best end I cowld bring him untow and therfor my deare
child at such tymes as the said les is ended take the sam into
yor owne handes or otherwyes lett the sam for a yearly rent
by resone it leeth a myle from you. It was parsell of yor
demane and allwas belonged to the hole by reson the demane
is but small, but in my openeone the only waye is to lett
the sam for a yearely rent, for I tak it that the sam grondes
wyll mak you twente markes a year, for so would it have
maid at such tymes as I bowg the said landes, which was in
the yeare of ower Lord God 1595. The sam was taken
from this houes by a forfetore for money lent upon en-
trest, therfor you maye be the more bowld to take the sam
at sych tyme as it shall fall, and ther is belongeng 2 or 3
hossus that stand opon the said land, the which is passed
in the sam les. Lok to them. And olso ther was more of

---

[1] 'mak him' struck out, 'a' inadvertently left in.

the sam land that Mr Wynstanley passed awaye, that is to
saye, Richard Orrell houes, Myles Wynstanleys howes and
Jhon Wynstanleys houes, Lore Farreclok houes and what
more I well kno not, whech were parsell of the said Har
Houes Grond, for as I am informed it contened abowt fyffe
acares and therfor you maye be the more bold, but I wold
not wych you to olter or chang ane of them but at such
tymes as the shall fall. Lett them go for reson, for so I hold
it best and the most godlyst.

[fo. 12r.]

My deare and loving childrene loke vere carfullye untow
this my advartesment in Gods most holye name that whatsoever landes it shall pleaies God tow send you by me youre
carfull Father, I straittlye charge you in Gods most holye
name that you never make ane leais tow ane of youere
tenant for ane longger tyme then for twente and on yeare,
for so shall you find thearein greatt profitt and gane tord
the advancesment of yor estaitt, and for that it shall the
more manefeast apeare unto you that my consell is just and
trowe, wheare the rent of the maner of Wynstanley is
abowte forte markes a yeare, in takyng this my consell you
shall mak yearely at the leaist fore skower pondes a yeare
in fines above the anchant rent, and so you shall take nothing but that which shall be resonabyll bowth in the sight
of God and the world, and so you shall pleaes yor tenantes
and be well spoken of, and two the end you shall the
better understand the same I have heare sett downe evere
manes tenement, the content of the acares and the rent
yearly and what it was worth at such tymes as I sett this my
derecone downe for youre good as herafter on the other
sid of the leaf apereth in the yeare of owere Lord God
1600

James Bankes

[fo. 12v.]

The names of the tenantes in Wynstanley and everemans
fyn what mor or les is worth to be sould unto the tenantes as
foloith—

Wyllam Barton of the cole pitt his tenement conteneth
abowt thrite[1] akers *or more* and is worth a yeare above the
rent twente pondes so that a leaies of the same is worth for
twente and on yeares a hondreth and twente pondes[2] and
thearefor my children if at ane tyme you can bye the said

li.

120–0

---

1 'forte' struck out.
2 'and thre skower' struck out, 'and twente' interlineated.

tenement for money not horting ane of his sones by the sam
and laie the same to yor demane you maye be bowld to geve
for the same 100*li.* for so it is worth vere well.

Robart Wynstanle of the mylne his tenement conteneth
about xviii acares and is worth above the rent six[1] ponds

30–0–0   the yeare so that a leas is worth to be sowld to the tenant
threte ponds[2] for the tearme of on and twente yeares. *In
ane wyes hourt not ane of his childrene of ther leais.*

Wyllam Barton at the far end of the towne his tenement
and now Crones hat a leaes thereof conteneth abowt fitte acares
and is worth above the rent xx*li.*[3] ponds a yeare so that a

200–0–0   leais is worth of the sam *for skower and tene ponds*[4] for the
tow   tearme of on and twente yeares.
hondreth
pondes   *If it pleaies God you my sone that you can bye in the said les of
Wyllam Crones, devid the same into fore or fyfe partes and lett by
a yearely rent and mak them lesses for iii lyfes and so shall you
find it most for yor profitt.*

[fo. 13r.]

Robart Wynstanley of the Sandeforth his tenement
conteneth abowt thrite and fife acares and is worth above
the aunchant rent *twenty markes*[5] a yeare so that a leaies is

li.   worth to be sould to the tenant 80[6] pondes,[7] for so I dowe
100–0–0   esteme them to be well worth, the which is abowt thre[8]
ponds an acar *fine.*

*This les is worth fore skower pondes for a fine, that is to saie,
thre pondes an aker fine.*

li.   Richard Orrell his tenement conteneth abowt fiftene[9]
20–0–0   acars and is worth above the rent xi*li.* a yeare so that a leais
is worth to be sowld to him or his for the tearme of xxi
yeares fore skower pondes,[10] *for Mr Wynstanley did tak for a
fine fyfte ponds for it.* Never mak ane les therof but lett the
sam at a yerly rent.[11]

Lawrances Farcloke his tenement conteneth abowt fitte[12]
100–0–0   acares and is worth by yeare above the rent twente ponds[13]
so it is worth a hondreth[14] ponds to ane mane. *I maid a les of
the sam for thrte ponds opon the sorendring in of a nowld les for ii*

---

[1] 'eyght' struck out.
[2] Substituted for 'thre skower and foure pondes'.
[3] 'twente' struck out, 'forte' interlineated and then struck out.
[4] This valuation has been substituted for an earlier one.
[5] 'fyfte pondes' struck out.   [6] 'a hondreth & twente' struck out.
[7] 'which is viii yeares fine' struck out.   [8] 'for' struck out.
[9] 'abowt thrittene' struck out.
[10] 'fower skower & five pondes' struck out.
[11] This sentence added as an afterthought.   [12] 'forte' struck out.
[13] 'fore pondes so that a leais' struck out. [14] 'fore skore and twelfe' struck out.

lyefes then to come, the which myght have contenued for manie yeares.

Jhon Wod by the capell his tenement conteneth twente acares and is worth above the rent twente markes[1] ayeare.

li.
100–0–0
li.
100–0–0

He hath maid of the same farme a hondreth ponds a yeare by reson he marled the same of aleven acares of barlye and therfor my deare children never les the sam anie more for he toke the forfetour being paid to him.

At such tymes as the money should have bene payd to Jhon Wod he would not tak the same but tok the forfetower of the tenement, therfor tak the sam agane or let it at the full rent or worth therof. Jhon Wods tenement is for iii lyfes mayd but if ever it fall take the sam into yor one handes, fale me not herein.

[fo. 13v.]

li.
100–0–0

Edmond Atharton his tenement conteneth abowt 26 acares and is worth twente marks a yeare above the rent so that a les therof is worth a hondreth[2] pondes vere well.

For theese tow leses, that is to say, Homfre Winstanleys lese and Wydoe Athertons, upon the determination of theme boethe to by theme in if it bee possible.

li.
100–0–0

Homfre Wynstanley his tenement conteneth 26 acares and is worth twente markes a yeare above the rent so that a les is worth a hondreth[3] pondes vere well and therfor tak no les.

This sayed Ofeye Winstanlei must decetefullie dide goe aboute as hee confessethe at suche tims as the land was to be sould and therefore deserveth no faver.

Roger Adlington his tenement contenes abowt eigtene acares and is worth a yeare viii[4] pondes above the rent so that a les is worth to be sould to him *forte and viiili.[5] The same*

li.
48–0–0

you maie tak into yor owenes handes not ofendyng God, for he tok a les over a power wones hed and most ungodly dailt wyth her and so turned her owt and hir children. [6]

li.
12

Gelbart Bebe his tenement and his cottler smythhie is worth three pondes a yeare. Ther is abowt[7] three acares of land to the sam.

li.
43–0–0

Thomas Orrell of the Broke his tenement contenes eig acares and is worth a yeare vj*li.*[8] pond xiij*s.*[9] so that the les is well worth forte markes[10] and thearefor if at ane tyme if it

[1] 'ponds' erased and 'markes' substituted in a later hand and in a different ink.
[2] 'and tene' struck out.   [3] 'and tene' struck out.
[4] 'nene' struck out.   [5] 'fower skower pondes' struck out.
[6] A later hand has crossed out the whole of this entry.
[7] 'aneare' struck out.   [8] 'vjli.' written over an erasure.
[9] 'vis. 8d.' struck out.   [10] 'pondes' struck out.

wylbe soueld by the sam and lait it to youre demane. Fale not herin in Godes name, it is worth 26–13–4.

*Let hime pay v*li. *yerely.*

[fo. 14r.]

Margrett Ranford her tenement contenes abowt viii acares and is worth abowt fyfe pond vi*s.* viii*d.*[1] is it worth a leas 26–0–0—I wowld have you to by the sam lykwyes if it be possibyll and laie the sam to yor demane, but in ane wyes dow no wrong to the houes of Raneford or two ane of his childrene becaues the name of the father and the sones have done good sarvis to this houes of Wynstanley, and if you can by the sam, plaies them in some other tenement, in Godes name—of the lyk or better in ane wyes. *A les of this houes as abovesaid is worth forte markes for won and twente yeares.*[2]

li.
26–6–8

Gelbart Barton his tenement contenneth abowth tene[3] acares and is worth a yeare if it be marled at the leaist fyfe pondes[4]—10.0—and thearefore my deare child by the sam and lait to youer demane and plaies him at some other tenement as well as you cane. Ther is abowt ij or thre acares that was taken from the demane, therfor if ever the leais be determened in ane wyes tak the same iij acares agane to the demane agane. As I tak it is caled the Hostid Hed. It leeth next to the lees on the farther sid of the heige.

li.
30–0–0

I have maid him a leies of the Hostid Hed and a little more. At my deth it faleth to the houes againe.

li.
2–0–0

Rauefe Berre hath a cotig in the sid of the demane and of the demane. I would lykewyes have you to tak the sam into youre handes at his deth and his wyfes and all the cotages abowt the mylne, for the dow hinder this houes mor then a man wold thinke.

[fo. 14v.]

Alexander Rilondes his tenement conteneth abowt viij acares besides the on halfe of the mylne, the which[5] is worth viij*li.* the yeare above the rent so that a leas of the sam is worth forte[6] pondes. By this if it be possibyll becaues it lieth in the demane and within the ring yard.[7]

li.
40–0–0

Homfre Atharton his tenement contenes thre acares demy and is worth above the rent forte shelengs[8] a yere

---

[1] 'forte and tow pondes 6*s.* 8*d.*' struck out.

[2] A later hand has crossed out the whole of this entry. The Rainford family was of Winstanley and Liverpool.

[3] 'iij' struck out. [4] 'fyfe pondes' and 'twente markes' both struck out.

[5] 'is the which' struck out. [6] 'thre skower and foure' struck out.

[7] Immediately after this an entry has been started in error and then struck out and intentionally blurred. [8] 'if it be marled forte [?] markes' struck out.

PLATE TWO   Susan Bankes, wife of James Bankes. Died 1627/8. Artist unknown

PLATE THREE

William Bankes
(1593–1666)
Artist unknown

above the rent. The land is vere good and becaues it lyeth wythin the ring yard you maye be bold to geve him for his leais tene pondes, for so it is well worth. A les is worth to be sould of this tenement *fyftene pondes.*

li.
13–6–8

Roger Ranford his tenement contenes abowt eygtene acares and is worth above the rent vi*li.* [1]pondes a yeare and therfor my deare sones by the sam and laie it unto yor demane. It lith wythin the ring yard and hath bene taken from the demane, besides six more which lyeth wythin the ring yard, that is to saie, Thomas Orrels of the Broke, the lor mylne, Ranford, Adlyngton, Barton, Met and Athartons, Rechard Wynstanles, all thes bi them and[2] [fo. 15*r.*] plaies them in som other as good tenementes in Gods most holye nam fale not herin, but if ane man would parswaid you to the contrare he is not yor frend, for so asure yorselfe so shall you be abyll to kype a power houes the better, and in Good most holye nam be a contenewall marler of yor demane, so shall you ries to good abelete and be abyll to porches to the incresing of yor houes, yor wyfe and children. Fale me not herin, yor carfull and loving Father,

James Bankes

Marle that which was never afor marled and no more medil not wythall in ane wyes, the charg is grett therin.

Margrett Bircholl hath a clois abowt fife *or six akers* acares the which the loird of this houes dyd *porchas of*[3] on Mr Worsley of Pemarton to the end to laye the sam to his demane becaues it litheth in Wynstanley and senen to the hole and for the sam gave him for the sam clois dobyll so mych land for the sam, therefor my deare son take the same at the deaith of the said Margrett into yor owene handes. It is all cole and vere good *as I am informed.* In the name of God folo this my advices in all cases that I shall sett you done in this boke.

Mylies Wynstanley his tenementes conten six acars and is worth above the rent thre[4] ponds a yeare which is worth to a leais[5] therof twente fore ponds. I have maid a les of this tenement for iii lyfes, therfor tell the sam be determened you can dow nothing.[6]

24–0–0

[fo. 15*v.*]

Necolas Crosse his tenement is worth abowt fouer pondes

---

[1] 'if it be marled at least thirte [?]' struck out.
[2] A later hand has crossed out all this entry as far as the end of this folio.
[3] 'paing [?] with' struck out.   [4] 'fore' struck out.
[5] 'sould' struck out.   [6] A later hand has crossed out the whole of this entry.

a yeare above the rent and the said Necolas Crosse payd for
the sam tene pondes and therfor opon the deaith of the said
Necolas and his wyfe by in the sam agane and ether kipe

the sam in yor owne hands and marle the sam or eles

remove som of the tenantes that lieth wythin the ringe
yarde to it. Fale nott herin for by this mene you maie
incres yor demane. The said tenement is worth to paye for
a fine *xx*li.[1] ponds for xxi yeres.

> *After the decese of the saide Niccolas Crossey and his wyfe there
> is tenne poundes to bee payed within a haulfe yere and see that
> it bee payed in the name of God, for otherwise the lese stands
> good during a younge mans life.*

Griaces of Colye[2] next untow Necolas Crosse her tenement
contene abowt tene acars besides the more and is worth

above the rent abowt fyfe pondes a yeare. A les to be maid

to ane man is worth *thrite ponds.*[3]

Thomas Chadoke his tenement contene thrite acares of
cowers land and som god and is worth the rent viii*li.* a
yeare. The same tenement is good if it wear marled and
therfor my deare son by the sam or ane other of the tene-

mentes at ane tyme if the said tenantes wyll sele[4] and fale

not in Goods most holye nam but tak none of them unles
you may have them wyth a fre conseanes in Good most
hole name.

[fo. 16r.]

Wyllam Penington haith a clois the which contenes abowt
thre acars or fore of the Har Houes Grond the which he
paieth for the sam fife sheleng rent and it is worth forte
sheleng a yeare and therfor opon the endyng of the said leais
tak the sam into yor on handes for Mr Wynstanley dyd this
houes grett wrong in letteng ane part of the Har Houes

Grond to ane person and therfor my deare children as the

lessus of ane part of the Hare Houes Ground the lessus
determyne take the same into yor handes tow the mantenanes of yor houes in Good name for yor good, for the same
Har Houes Ground dyd allwais belong to the hole of
Wynstanley, or eles les them owtt as I have apointed for the
tearme of won and twente yeares and not above whatsoever
les you make.[5]

Richard Wynstanley his tenement contene abowt thre
acares and a halfe and is vere good land if it were marled it

---

[1] 'therte' struck out.   [2] 'but now James Horson' struck out.
[3] 'thrite and iij pondes' struck out.   [4] 'the sam' struck out.
[5] A later hand has crossed out the whole of this entry.

wyll bring you in at the leaist fyfe[1] pondes *and more* a yeare and therefor by in the leais and marle the sam. In ane wyes it is worth forte sheleng a yeare above the rent if you can by the leais. Rather then fale geve for the sam twente nobles *or ten pondes* for so it is *well worth.*[2] A les is worth for xxi yeres . . .[3]

li.

13–6–8

[fo. 16*v*.]

    Robart Atharton hath a fild coled the Cros Fild which is abow two acars or mor the which he paieth xii*d.* a yeare and is worth *thre pones* a yeare above the rent and cam by the sam most ungodlye for after that I haid bowght the land of Mr Wynstanley he most conningly went to Mr Wynstanley and for nothing procowred him to mak him a leais for thre lyfes contrare tow all Christen delings, the which said leais was worth for thre lyfes twente ponds and therfor my child if you can by in the leais rather then fale geve him for the sam twente nobiles[4] for so is it well worth. He hath maid of it in a yeare being sone wyth wheat at the lest sixten ponds and therfor my child never leais the sam agane for it is parsell of the Hare Houes Grond. This same Crost Fild wyll mak you won yere wyth another at the les for markes a yeare for ever if it be sone twyes in tene yeares, therfor part not wyth it. *This Croies Fild wyll mak you at the lest fyfe markes a yeare.*

three
pones a
yeare

li.

20–0–0

    James Pinington hath a letell clois next to the Crois Fild for the which he paieth vi*d.* a yeare, parsell of the Har Houes Grond, the which he gave me twente sheleng for a fyne and at such tymes as the leais is determened laie the sam to the Cros Fild and take them into yor owen handes to incres yor demane, for so maye you be abyll to kype the better houes.[5]

li.

1–0–0

[fo. 17*r*.]

    Loure Fareclok her tenement contenes fore acares and is worth forte sheleng a year bove the rent and the same tenement is of the Har Houes Grond and therfor opon the determenacone of the leaes tak the sam into yor hands. A leais for xxi yeres of the sam is worth fifte[6] ponds and so you maye have for the sam.

li.

50–0–0

    Jhon Wynstanley the elder who dweleth opon the Har Houes Ground his tenement conteneth abowt thre acars or better and is worth above the rent forte sheling a yeare. The man is power.[7] A les is worth sixten ponds for xxi yeres

li.

16–0–0

---

[1] 'fyfe' overwritten on erasure.   [2] 'worth' struck out.
[3] 'twente [illegible]' struck out.   [4] 'twente nobiles' superimposed on erasure.
[5] A later hand has crossed out the whole of this entry.   [6] 'forte' struck out.
[7] 'and therfor plaies him in some other plaies and take the sam into youre one handes' struck out.

but if his son wyll geve you tene pondes for the sam lett him or his have it. He is a power man. Lett him remane and his sid.

Wyllam Bartone of the Browne Heath his tenement conteneth abowt sixtene acares roght and smouth land and is worth a yeare four pondes above the rent. The said Wyllam is a baid man and hath desavid me in taking of his tenement of Mr Wynstanley but his son maye prove well and therfor be good to his child.

li.
20-0-0

Jhon Farhorst tenement is worth thrite sheleng a year above the rent and as I tak it about an acar and a halfe. He tok a les after I bowg the land and so cosened me before my asuranes was maid and lykwyes Robart Atharton at the capell, *therefor in ane wyes when Athertons les is owt take the same into your one handes. Take into youre one hands Robart Athartons Crose Feld for he is a most baid man and cosend me.*[1]

li.
10-0-0

[fo. 17v.]

Jhon Gaskell[2] his tenement *is about 12 akers*[3] and is worth a yeare above the rent xii pones[4] so that a leais of the sam is worth forte pondes for the tearme of won and twente yeares. *It is worth the leais forte pones. Never lett ane les but in this sort for a yerly rent for it wyll mak you a yeare 12li.*

li.
80-0-0

When this lese is determened the same never to bee letten but at a fulle yerely rente.

Henrie Graie his tenement contenes abowt sixtene acars and is worth above the rent abowt *fife*[5] ponds a yeare so that a leas of the sam is worth thrite pondes for the tearme of won and twente yeares.

This tenement of Henre Graies wyll in short tyme come to yor handes and therefor I would advies you to by in the sam and to plaies som of the tenantes wythin the ring yard opon the sam. Fale not herin for so you maye incres youre demane in good sort.

If ever this tenemente faule the same never to bee letten.

Elizabeth Grene *and now Edmond her sone* her tenement contenes above fyfe acares and is worth above the rent fortie sheleng.[6] A les of the sam is worth tene ponds vere well for the tearme of twente and wone yeares.

li.
10-0-0

Jhon Horst a houes wyth a gardyn and an all smethe wyth som small land abowt the smethe for the which he payeth a mark of the owld anchant rent the which I well think is

---

[1] A later hand has crossed out the whole of this entry.
[2] 'Jon Gaskell' struck out.
[3] 'contenes abowt syxtene acares', 'fortene', 'or xiij' all struck out.
[4] 'four' and 'xij*li*.' both struck out.
[5] 'fore' struck out.   [6] 'a yeare' struck out

li.
10–0–0

worth thrite sheleng a yeare. A les therof for xxi yeares is worth about ten pones.[1]

If this shall fale you ma lett it for a yerly rent at thre pondes the yeare.

[fo. 18r.]

Jhon Wynstanleye the yonger his tenement contene about

li.
8–0–0

six acares of cors land and is worth above the rent abowt twente sheleng a yeare. A les for xxi yeares is worth eight pondes.

Jhon Acowlye hi howldeth a clois of land of myne lying

li.
12–0–0

in *Wynstanley*[2] as I think conteneing about thre acares or skant which is wor a leais of the sam abott xii*li*. It is worth a yeare thrite shelengs *above the rent. Lett this when it shall plaies God at a yerly rent as it is worth.*

The feeled of John Cooley to be letten at a fulle yerely rente.

Rauefe Berre hath a coteg and a small parsell of grond the

li.
1–0–0

which he paieth *iii*[3] sheleng a yeare. Opon the detarmyna- cone of the leas take the sam into yor handes by resone it lyeth in the demaine. Fale not my deare child.[4]

An Clarkesone a cotege for thre lyfes the which is worthe above the rent tene sheleng a yeare. A leais is worthe four

li.
4–0–0

ponde for the terme of won and twente yeares but in no wyes asent to mak ane leaies by reson the hous standeth in the ring yard and wythin the demaine and otherwyes you shalbe grettly hendred by thes coteges.

If ever this faulle parte of it to bee preserved for a colliers house.

Thomas Darbeshere and Elyn Darbshere hat ather a coteg. I lykwyes forwarne you my deare child that after ther departoure to pole done thes thre coteges as I apoint you and olle other hosus thet lyeth in yore ring yard the open the obtening of the tenementes into yor handes.

This in licke maner to bee reserved for a collier.

[fo. 18v.]

Rechard Tomsone hath a coteg wythin the ring yard and if you can plaies his sone after him owt of the demane plaices him and pole downe the houes and all other of the howsus that lyith wythin the ring yard opon the detarmena- con of ther lessus for feare ther be newe hosus arected wythin the ring yard *a gud Gods nam.*[5]

This same house to bee reserved for a collier.

---

[1] A later hand has crossed out the whole of this entry.

[2] 'Bellyng' struck out. Probably an enclave in Billinge of a detached part of Winstanley Hence the change in the manuscript.   [3] 'fore' struck out.

[4] A later hand has crossed out the whole of this entry.   [5] This addition is not highly legible. Most of this side of the folio has been deliberately obliterated.

[fo. 19r.]

James Talyer of Orrell he hath a cotig and ther remaneth to hitt in land abowt an acar[1] or therabowt for the which he *li.* path iiii*s.* a yeare and it is worth a mark or fyften sheleng a 5–0–0 yeare. A les of the sam for won and twente yeares is worth abow fyfe ponds.

li. Robart Farremane hath a cotig in Orrell and it is worth a 1–0–0 les for xxi yeres twente sheleng.

li. Homfre Talyer lekwyes hath a cotig in Orrell and a 1–0–0 leaies is worth twente sheleng for the lyk tyme.

li. James Hamsone hath a coteg wythin the demane and a 2–0–0 leaies is worth for xxi yeares a fine of the sam . . . Opon the endying of the leais pole done the houes. Lett no coteges reman in your demane.

This never to bee altered.

li. s. Homfre Molenex hat a cotig which is worthe above the 1–12–0 rent fore sheleng a yeare. A les for wone and twente yeares is worth threte and two shelengs.

Thomas Farecloke his tenement contenes abowt eig acares and is worth a leas for won and twente yeares eig 8–0–0 ponds. The land is vere coures.

Mye deare childrene in all yor cauesus whatsoever you take in hand dow the same in the feare of God and then refar the sucses to God. Amen. I pras God.

[fo. 19v.]

Mystris Sherington *is now ded and the sam is las to Jhon Sherington* hath a les of my houes in Pemerton the which she paid for a les for thre liefes the som of two hondreth thre skowere and tene pondes the which is better then the rent *li.* be twente pondes a yeare. A les for won and twente yeares 200–0–0 is worth tow hondreth ponds and I think it is no more worth tho she paid so mych.

Unto Peter Orrell whom I sould it unto this les my aunt Sherington hat geven it tow my[2] boies Tomas[3] paiing forth of the sam tene pondes a yeare durring the lyf of on Domford a cosin of heres.

Necolas Nalyer of Orrell hath a les the which is tene *li.* pondes a yeare above the rent. A leais is worth of the sam 60[5]–0–0 for wone and twente yeares thre skower[4] pondes. *Never lett this houes wherin Jhon Nalyer dwellet but for a yerly rent for I*

---

[1] 'and a half' struck out or intended so to be.   [2] 'tow' struck out.
[3] 'and Raufe' struck out.
[4] 'and sixtene' struck out.
[5] '60' superimposed on erasure.

*dow tak it wyll mak you abowt xii*li. *a yere besids the benifitt of the cole pitt.*

li. s. d.
3–6–8

Thomas Wettnoll hath a cotig wythin the demane. Plaies him in som other plaies as sone as you cane. A les of his houes is worthe for xxi yeares fyfe markes but in no wyes mak ane les.

This when it fauls to be reserved for a colliers house. J.B.

Jane Wynstanley hath a letell tenement abowt fore acares the which is worth above the rent forte sheleng a yeare and a leais of the sam is worth sixtene pondes olltho

16–0–0

I dyd tak but fyfe pondes for xxi yeares.

When this les shall fawle lett the sam for a yerly rent. My dere childrene[1] if God shall send you to be lordes of ane tenantes se that you never make ane les above won and twente yeres for so shall you kipe yor tenantes in good and dowtefull obedeinces tow you and all mene.

[fo. 20r.]

Lands in Wystone coled Rodgatt parsell of the deman wyth the tenantes as hereafter foloith:— *These landes I have sould.*[2]

li.
10–0–0

Thomas Wodfall abowt iii acares. His tenement is worth twente sheleng a yere above the rent. A leas of the sam is worth tene pondes for xxi yeare.

li. s. d.
5–6–8

Robart Lowe his tenement is abo ii acars and is worth abowt a marke a yeare above the rent. A leais of the sam is worth for the tearme of xxi yeares fyfe–6–8.

6–0–0

Roger Whittfild his tenement contenes abowt tow acares and is worthe fyftene sheleng above the rent a yeare. A les is worth for the tearme of won and twente yeares six pondes.

5–6–8

Catrin Holond her tenement is worth a yeare above the rent abowt fyfteen sheleng. A leais of the sam is worth abowth fyfe pondes–6–8.

6–13–4

Edmond Farehourst hes tenement contene abowt ii acares or more and is worth above the rent abowt fiftene sheleng a yere above the rent. A leais of the sam for xxi yeares is worth six pond 13*s.*–4.

5–6–8

Gorg Inces his tenement contenes abowt tow acares and is worth above the rent abowt a marke a yeare. A leais for won and twente yeares is worth fyf ponds 6–8.

I have sould this land agane.

[fo. 20v.]

Wyllaim Ackers his tenemente contenes abowt ii acars and

---

[1] 'child' struck out.
[2] A later hand has crossed out each entry on this and the succeeding folio.

6–13–4   a halfe and is worth abowt sixten sheleng a yeare above the rent. A les for won and twente yeares is worth abowt six pond thrte sheleng four pentes.

            Jane Webstare a cotig wyth a gardyne thre sheles foure

0–3–4   pences the which is rent sofesint for the sam.

li. s .d.   The rents of the eyght tenantes is of Rodgatt

2–9–4

	s	d
The chif rentes of Rodgaitt is..............	0	3	2
Elzabeth Cottram hir chif rent is..........	0	1	0
Gorge Rachdall......................	1	1	10
Gorg Tomson........................	0	0	4*d.*

            Besides the tenantes of Wyston is to send evore on of them tow dayees shereing from evre houes tow Wynstanley during ther leaissus but becaues it is fearre for them tow come I would have you my son tow tak money of them, that is to saie, tow grott apices which som is in mony fyfe

li. s.   shelengs iiii so the som of the rent is of the tenantes in rents

12–11–8   and sarvic wyth the mylne and the demane land which is lett for viii*li.* a yere and the mylne fyf nobyles a year besides the cole pitt is in peine[1] rent twelfe pondes aleaven shelengs viii*d.*

    Ther is more chif rentes fond at Rodgatt as foloith
[fo. 21r.]
     Chiffe rentes at Rodgatt as foloith herafter

	s	d
Gorge Rachdall his chife rent is..........	0	1	10
Elezabeth Cokerom her chife rent is......	0	1	0
Mr Jhon Ogells his chife rent is..........	0	0	4*d.*
Mr Peter Wetherbe his chife rent is....	0	0	2*d.*
Gorge Tomlynsone his chife rent is........	0	0	4

This land I sould agane.
[fo. 22r.]
     My deare cheldrene I would have you to make as mych tillaig as possibyll you allwayes cane and to gett corne for therin is the most profitt of hosbanre for in bredyng of cattel is grett los and mak tyllaig of yor best land that is good and therin yor gane wylbe grettist, for corne is rede mone and cometh ones a yeare and be allwas as you can marlyng yor ground. Lett not anie man parswaid you to the contrare in Godd most hole name. Amen. And in oll yor acones fere

---

[1] doubtful reading, for 'penny' or 'paying'.

God and he wyll derecke yor afaire both tow God and the world.

Yor carfull Father
James Bankes

Brid no beais but ollwais by yong steres of 2-yeares owld and then you shall by a yok for fyf ponds or therabowt and when you have kepe them 2[1] yeres sel them and the wyll mak you a yoke abowt viii*li*. or parhapes mor. Kype no mor horsis then you most nedes in Gods name.

[fo. 22*v.*]

My deare childrene I straitlye charg you in the nam of God that you dow nothing that is contrare to the law of God for asure yorselfes whathsoevver is done to the contrarrie it wyll never stand but God wyl ponich you for the sam ether won waye or other and that you shall never understand it but if you in oll your doing feare God he wyll bles yor prosiding in which I praye God you maye and yor children to the ende of the world. Amen.

Yor carrfull Father
James Bankes

And forthermore my dear and eldest sone Wyllaim I would have if it shall pleais God tow send you issu of yor bodie that in ane wyes if God send yo a sone to name him James and so the eldest sone of this houes allwayes to name his eldest son James and my reson is this that wher it plesed God tow bles me yor Father and that by Gods good wyll and plesuer dyd advannes my name in the obtening of this maner of Wynstanley by my grett indistre and travell all the daies of my yong yeres which was vere charabyll to me yor most carfull father [fo. 23*r.*] I therefor straitly charg you to obsarve this my derecone in the naming of yor eldest sone James and in serving God he wyll bles oll yor prosiding and if you do the contrare and fer not God he wyll then overthro yor houes as he did this before I bowght the sam, for if Mr Edmond Wynstanley haid servd God I haid never bowght this land and so my dere children in oll youer afaires fer God and your houes God saith shalbe blessed to the end of the world, the which I praye God to contenew to his gracewes wyll and plesur. Amen.

Yor carfull Father
James Bankes[2]

---

[1] '3 or 4' struck out.
[2] This marks the end of the original. The remainder was added a few years later.

Wedo Birchall
Tomas Orrell of the Brok
Alixsonder Rilones
owld Ranfordes wyfe
Roger Adlington
Roger Ranford
Tomas Harreson, which was Harre Graies houes
Wyllam Crones
Robart Atharton
Wyllam Peningtons
Necolas Crosse
Jhon Wod
Jhon Nalyer in Orrell
Jhon Sherington in Pemarton
Jhon Warnesley in Howton

My son Wyllam you maie tak into youre handes all thes tenantes that I have sett you downe as above said, not ofendyng God, that is to saie, Wedo Bircholl, Roger Adlington, Roger Ranfordes, Tomas Haresones, Wyllam Crunes, Robart Atharton, Wyllam Penington, Necolas Crosse, Jhon Wod, Jhon Naler, Jhon Sherington, Jon Warnley in Howton, oll thes you maie lafully tak into yor handes opon the detarmenacone of there lessus and yett olltho you maie by the law of this land take the sam I [fo. 23*v*.] would geve you resones to evere one whi you maie dow the sam and my first resone is that for Birchall leies wherein ther is but one lyvefe to come and the les ended, you maie bouldly tak the sam not ofending God by reson ther was an exchang maid betwene my cossin Worsley and Mr Wynstanley of a woud ajoining to the sam fild wherin was vere god timber and sarten closus of grownd besides at the lest tweies so mych in thope Mr Wynstanley should find a good myne of coles and so he was desavid in the exchang, therfor in Gods nam tak the sam into youre handes and ther is marell good store to marl the sam and it wyll mak you at the lest fiften pondes a yeare, therfor my dere son never lett the sam agane by lese by no parshaqune of ane man whatsoever in this caies shall move you, so shall you incres yor demane, which is but small for the mantening of yor houes. In Godes name I advies you herunto to folo my derecone herin and not to fale me herof, for you maie lafuly do the sam by the laies of God.

At such tymes as I bowg this land coled the maner of Wynstanley ther was a les maid by Edmond Wynstanley of

a tenement tow Roger Adlington and as sone after I haid
bowght the said lands of Mr Edmond Wynstanley, this
said Roger Adlington torned the said tenant owtt of the
houes and hir sone, the which browght the power wedow
intow a meserabyll astaitt and want to her utter and grett
loues and ollmost undoing, therfor my deaire son at such
tymes as the said tenement shall fawll to yor handes tak the
[fo. 24r.] sam into youre owne handes, for the said Roger is a
most baid man sondre waies and so apparranly knowe of oll
his nebores and as it is thowght well not mend and therfor tak
the sam into yor owne handes and never lett the sam agane
to ane man but lai the sam to yor demane, for so you maye
lafully dow both by Gods laies and the kings, I wyll asure
you herein

J. B.

And lykwyes her is another tenement the which was taken
over a power wedowes hed, won Chadokes wyfe, by Ranfor
in the lyk sorrt for thre lyfes wherein is in the houldyng of
won Roger Ranford and his mother. Opon the detarmenacone of the les tak the sam into yor owne handes or befor
by in his titell if it be possibyll. I think the sam is well worth
thrite pondes. It joneth to yor demane, and so shall you
not in takyng of the sam after the endyng of dow him no
wrong but justis both by equete and right to bowth sides.

J. B.

And lykwyes ther is another tenement wherin won Wyllam
Crones dyd tak over a pore man hed to his ondoing of him
and his wyfe and childrene, wheropon the pore man wyfe
deed for vere grefe, the which Crones pout them owt by the
shrefe and so the pore man Barton, whomes name was, was
constraned to mak a pore cabin wythowt the houes and
inforsed to lye opon the grownd a howle wynter, stell in
hope of som relife at the said Crones his hand, but no pete
would he geve her in ane sort and in the behalfe of the
power man his nebores in the end releved him wyth begeng,
otherwyes he showed have bene inforsed to have beged for
wan of relyfe, therfor my sone [fo. 24v.] if you can by in this
leaies and lett the powere man have the said houes agane
doring his lyf if he shall lif after me yor father, in God most
holy name. He desireth but a dosen acares therof doring his
lyvefe. This said Wyllam Crones hath a lese doring his lyf
and for fower skowr yeres if he leve so long. The said les Mr

Wynstanley bestoid it on him wytoten[1] ane pene for the sam. Therfor in in regard it cost him nothing, he myght have gevven some relyfe to the said pore man, but his hart woud not soffer him to dow so mych good. The tenement is abowt fyftie acares as I am informed of cowerse land and I hould it is worth abowt ten pondes above the rent, and if it shall pleaies God that you maie obtene the same then you maie plaies som of youer tenantes that lieth nere you opon part therof and so incres yore demane mor ner a you, which is the best for yor powere houes, but in God nam pleaies them wyth as mych as there be worth and rather the more, so shall you pleaies both God and them.

And lykwyes there is another tenant which was morgoghed by Mr Edmond Wynstanley two on of his tenantes, whomes nam in Jhon Wod, for a hondreth pondes redemabill at the plesure of Mr Wynstanley or his asines, the which was myselfe, James Bankes, the porchesser of the said maner of Wynstanley, and opon the porches so maid, I, the said James Bankes, would have paid the said hondreth pondes accordingly to the said Jhon Woid[2] who most shamfully denied to resave the same, and therfor at sych tymes as the said lees endeth tak the sam into youere handes. It is about twente acares or more and is worth fyftene ponds a yeare and is parsell of the demane land, therfor never lett the sam agane to ane man.

Let this when it fauls at a full yerely rent.   *J.B.*

[fo. 25r.]

Jhon Nalyer in Orrell hath taken a les of my land ther, that I bowg of wone Peter Orrell, most falesly, for contrare to all good deling beinge sett on by wone that hath bene a grett eneme to my wyfe and childrene, and therefore opone the endyng of the leaies tak the sam into yor owne hands. This baid felo being sett on kept me vii yeares from my rent by deviessus and in the end at the intrete of his frend I dyd abait him therof fyf markes, sines which tyme he hath hindred me,—and his ungodly frend—, xx*li.* at the lest in my colepitt, or otherwyes lett the sam for a yearly rent it wyll mak you at the lest[3] twenty markes a yere. Never les the sam but incres yor rent, in God name I advies you and tak hid you folo my consell in this behalfe.

When this lese shaulle faule let the sam at a fulle yerely rent.

J. B.

---

[1] Cf. Old English 'wiðutan.'   [2] Four words purposely obliterated here.
[3] 'tene pondes' struck out, 'twenty markes' inserted later.

[fo. 25v.]

Sines my sone that I did sett downe her in this bock my openine for the good of thie and thi posterrete, I have forther maid consetheracone for the benefitt of the and thoues that shall com after the and have found the sam moust for yor good by comen experiench and most sound prouef to my grett hindrennes and loies as apereith by my bok of acownt planly to be sine from yeare to yeare as foloith the greaitt charges that I have bene at in keping sarvantes to dow my hosbanre to my loise and henderances. Therfor my son in the name of God folow my consell herin. Mak no more tillaig to gett corne then to sarf your houes for, for I have bene hendered by keping of sarvantes in getting of corne that I have rather desired to deye then to lyf, for the car not whether end goeth forward so that the have mett, drink and wagues. Small feare of God is in sarvantes and thow shall find my consell just and most trew.

James Bankes

[fo. 26r.]

This advertesment was sett downe in the yeare of ower Loird God 1610—

My sone wheare I have advizaid thie to mak lessus when ane tenement shall fall, I have fond it by comon epeirins grettly to the contrare, therefor folow this my consell in the name of God, for so shalt thou be abyll to livefe if thou fearre God in all thi doinges, that is tow saie, when ane leaies shall fale to thie, lett the same to the tenant agane for a yearly rent and in Goids name tak not to mych rent nor yett tow lettell, for a mene is the best, so shalt thow be best abyll to life.

James Wynstanley of the Hare Melne his tenement contenes abowt sixtene akers besids the melne and is wor by yeare seven pondes. Lett the land and the milne together to
li.
v–0–0
him or his for fyfe pondes a yeare rent wythoten[1] anie fine for the same.

Wyllam Crones haith lett his tenement the which he haith under me for twente pondes a year above the rent, so
xxi*li.*
xiiii*s.*
the tenantes that he haith lett the same untow paith in rent xxi*li.* and xiiii*s.* a yeare besides ther sarvis, and so you maie lett the sam as he doith lafully. This leais Mr Wynstanley dyd geve the sam to Crones.

[1] Cf. Old English 'wiðutan'.

Wyllam Barton his tenement contenes aboitt thrte akers and is worth above the rent twente ponds a yeare.

xx*li.*

Robart Wynstanley his tenement contens abow xxx akers or more and is worth by yeare xvi pondes. When it falleth lett the same for ten pondes rent a yeare.

x*li.*

The som on this sid is 56–14–0.

[fo. 26*v.*]

Rechard Orrel his tenement contenes abowt sixtene akers and is worth by yeare abowt twelfe pondes, and when it faleth you maie lett the sam for viii*li.* a yeare. It was of the demane land.

viii*li.*

Lorances Farcloik his tenement contenes abowt fyfte akers and is worth be yeare xx*li.* You maie lett the same for xvi*li.* a yeare vere well.

xvi*li.*

Jhon Wod his tenement contenes aboitt xxiii akers and is worth by yeare abowt fyftene pondes. You maie lett the sam for tene pondes a yeare. The same land was of the demane.

x*li.*

Edmond Atharton his tenement contenes abowt xxvi akers and is worth by yeare fyftene poindes. You maie lett the same for twelf ponds a yer.

xii*li.*

Homfre Wynstanley his tenement contenes xxvi akers worth by yeare fyftene pondes. You maie lett the sam for xii*li.* when it shall falle.

xii*li.*

Roger Adlington his tenement contenes abowt xv acares and is worth by yeare seven pondes.[1]

vii*li.*

Tomas Orrell his tenement contenes abowt xii akers and is worth by yeare xii*li.* You maie lett the same well for viii*li.* a yeare.

viii*li.*

The Wedow Orreles of the Broke her tenement contenes abowt viii akers and is worth by yeare to be lett vi*li.*[1]

vj*li.*

Wyllaim Penington haith a medow of foure or fye akers worth by yeare forte shelenges.

ii*li.*

Harre Graie haith a tenement abowt xv akers worth by yeare abow fyf pondes.[2]

iiii*li.*

The som on this sid is 27–0–0.

[fo. 27*r.*]

Gelbart Barton his tenement contenes abowt tene akers worth by yeare to be lett

x*li.*[1]

James Acowlye his tenement contenes abowt twente akers worth by yeare abowt fyfe pondes.

v*li.*

Roger Ranford his tenement contenes abowt sixtene akers worth by yeare abowt

viii*li.*

---

[1] A later hand has crossed out the whole of this entry.
[2] 'fore pondes' struck out or intended so to be.

viiili.

Tomas Wynstanley his tenement contenes aboitt sixtene akers worth by yere fyfe pondes.

iiiili.

Wyllaim Barton of the Browne Heaith his tenement contenes xii akers worth a yeare... *This same tenement when it fauls to be let at a full yerely rent.*

viiili.

Tomas Chadok his tenement contenes abowt twente akers worth by yeare

iili. xiiis.

Lorances Farcloik his tenement iii[1] akers worth by yeare

iiiid.

iiiili.

Margrett Birchall a clois coled the Roigh Heiye worth by yeare abowt iiiili. the which heiye conteneth aboitt six akers and if the sam fild wer marled it were worth ten ponds by yeare.

iiiili.

Edmond Grene his tenement contenes aboit vi akres worth by yeare abowtt

xiili.

Tomas Gaskell his tenement contenes abowt ten akers worth by yeare

li.

Margrett Ranford her tenement contanes aboit seven

vi-o-

akers worth by yeare *sixe*[2] pondes.

The som on this sid 53–0–0

[fo. 27v.]

viili.

Alixsonder Rilonces his tenement contenes aboit viii akres and is worth[3] seven[4] pondes a yeare *besides the mylne. Never lett the mylne agane.*

xxxs.

James Wynstanley his tenement contenes abow thre akers worth by yare xxxs.

xxxs.

Robar Nalyer his tenement abowt six akers or mor worth by yeare thrte shelings.

xls.

Olevor Wethington haith a nale smethe and som smale laind theruntow beloingeng worth by yare forte sheleng and better.

xli.[5]

Wyllam Ranford his tenement contenes six akers worth by yeare

iiili.

Edmond Bebe his tenement aboitt iii akers wyth a smethe to mak knifes worth by yeare. *Never leitt the said thre akers for it is of the demane land as moust plainely apereth. iii akers to bee taken backe againe.*[6]

When this tenemente faulls let the same at a fulle yerely rente.

J. B.

xxxxs.

Edmond Atharton his tenement contenes thre akers worth by yare *ii ponds.*

The tenemente of Richard Winstanley after his deses to bee let out at a fulle yerely rente.

---

[1] 'v' struck out.   [2] 'fore' struck out.   [3] 'fyfe' struck out.
[4] 'with the milne' struck out.   [5] 'ten' overwritten 'seven'.
[6] 'v' struck out.   [7] Last sentence added later still.

xxx*s*.	Richard Wynstanley his tenement iii akers.
xiii*s*.	Jhon Wynstanley his tenement is abowt tene akers worth by yeare
xx*x*s.	Tomas Farcloik his tenement is abowt ten akers and worth by yeare
	Edmond Bebe his tenement on the mor sid abowt ten
xx*x*s.	akers worth by yeare. *The same feelde to bee letten iiij*li.
xxx*s*.	Jhon Acolye a fild abowt thre acares worth by yeare thrt shelengs.

The som on this sid is 30*li*.–o–o

[fo. 28r.]

Olever Hasselldeine hait a fild colud the Crois Fild of
iii*li*.   thre akers worth by yeare thre ponds.

The said cloies was desaifully gotten from this houes.
Therfor whin God shal send it to fall you maie lett the sam
for the most rent you can.

xxxi*s*.   Thourstan Farhorst haith a howes and a clois worth by
yeare

Necolas Crosse hath a tenement abow twente acares
*v*li. *J.B.*[1]   wherof ther is in god land abowt for or fyf acares and the rest
is in roug land worth by yeare abowt fore ponds.

Jane Wynstanley a houes and thre akers of land and
xxxx*s*.   worth by yeare

All thes tenantes that com after ar but cotoguis.

Rauef Talyer half an aker paing ten penes a yeare to him
x*d*.   and his ares for ever.

James Penington a small peces of land[2] the which I maid
vi*d*.   him a les of for the which he paieth six pences a yeare.

Rauefe Berre a howes and a garden for the which he paith
a yeare. . . But in ane wyes after the desese of them boith
iiii*s*.   tak done the hous and sel the timber therof. It standeth in
the demane.

Tomas Wetnoll a cotig.		v*s*.
Homfre Molenus a cotig at		ii*s*. the year
Harre Grene a cotig.		ii*s*. vi*d*.
Tomas Darbshere a cotidg.		ii*s*.
Rauefe Waitt a cotig.		ii*s*.
Homfre Tomson a cotige.		
James Hamson a cotige.		iiii*s*.

*The som on this sid is ii*li.–o–o

[fo. 28v.]

Roger Bebe a cotig wyth half anker[3]   ii*s*.

---

[1] 'iiii*li*.' struck out.   [2] 'paing' struck out.   [3] 'anaker' intended.

Ole the cotegus as the fall tak done the hosus and mak money of them, but houet none befor the fall to you in God name so be it.

My son I have wyth grett care sowght owt the best waie tow incres thi leving for the good mantenanes of thi powere houes the which by Gods helpe thou shalt find most assurdlye for thi good if thow folow this my carfull[1] dereccon. Ther is nene of the tenantes as foloith herafter which have but on lyvefe apices, that is to saie[2]

	li.
James Wynstanley of the mylne............	5–0
Wedow Orrell.........................	6–0–0
Roger Ranford........................	6–0–0
Lorranes Farclok......................	2–0–0
Margrett Birchall......................	4–0–0
Margrett Ranford......................	5–0–0
Alixsnder Rilones.....................	8–0–
Olever Hasselldeine	3–0–
Thes nene tenant wyl mak above the anchant rent thrite and won pondes a yeare........	31–0–0

By Godes helpe besides other that wyll fall whene it shall plaies God. *Ther is mor the which but on lyfeve apies Jhon Warnesley worth by yeare li. 30–0–. Bartons son of the Brone*
iiii*li.* *Heith won lyf to com worth by yeare*

[fo. 30r.]

Rogger Rainford his tenement contenes about sixtene
viii*li.* akers and is worth by yere
Peter Lyon worth more.

Thomas Winstanlie his tenement contenes aboute sixteene
viii*li.* akers and is worth by yere
Edmund Winstanley more worth.

William Barton his tenement contenes about xii akers and
iiii*li.* is worth by yere
Robert Wetherby more worth.

Thomas Chadocke his tenement contenes about twentie
viii*li.* akers and is worthe by yere
In severall hands.

Laurance Farcloch his tenement contenes about fore
iiii*li.* akers and is worthe by yere
Richard Fairclough

Margerit Burchaulle hathe a feeled of myne cauled Rid
iiii*li.* Hei the whiche is worthe by yere iiii pounds the which hei

---

[1] At this point 'and' has been mistakenly inserted.
[2] A later hand has crossed out the whole of the following table.

contenethe about seven akers and if the same were marled it were worthe ten pound a yere.

Edmond Greene his tenement contenes about vi akers
iii*li*.   and is worth by yere

In severall hands.

Thomas Gaschel his tenement contenes about ten akers
xii*li*.   and worthe by yere

John Gaskell

Thes eigh tenantes are worth by yeare 49 –o–

[fo. 30*v*.]

Margaret Rainford her tenement contenes about seven
vi*li*.   akers and is worthe by yere six poundes.

Robert Atherton more worth.

Alixsonder Rilons his tenement contenes about viii akers
vii*li*.   and is worthe by yere vii*li*. besides the milne. Never let the same out agane.

More worth.

vii*li*.   And the mylne is worth a yeare

James Wynstanley his tenement contenes about three
xxx*s*.   akers and is worth by yere

Robert Winstanley, Dennis Robin

Robert Nalier his tenement contenes about vi akers and is
xxx*s*.   worthe by yere

Peter Rainford

Olivere Weethingeton hathe a nale smithie and sum
xl*s*.   grounds belonging unto the same worthe by yere
v*li*.   William Rainforde his tenement contenes about sis akers
and is worthe by yere

George Rainford more acres more worth.

Edmond Bibbie his tenement contenes about three akers
withe a smithie to macke nives and is worthe by yere
iii*li*.   iii*li*. Never let the sade three akers againe for it is of the demane lands.

John Wilson

Thes seven tenant is worth by yeare 33 *li.*

THE PROBATE INVENTORY
OF JAMES BANKES
1617

A Just and True Inventory of all the goodes chatles and debts of James Bancks late of Winstanley in the Countye of Lancaster Esquior deceased praysed the 11th daie of Auguste Anno Domini 1617 by us Richard Billinge Christofer Robye Edmund Winstanley and James Scotte as followeth videlicet

Imprimis twoe yoke of oxen		xix*li*. iij*s*. iiij*d*.
Item foure yong bollocks		xj*li*. vj*s*. viij*d*.
,,	eighte calffes	vij*li*. x*s*. o
,,	seaventeen cowes	lj*li*. x*s*. o
,,	foure heffers	xj*li*. x*s*.
,,	three mares	xij*li*. xviij*s*. iiij*d*.
,,	twoe nagges	vij*li*.
,,	one colte	xxxiij*s*. iiij*d*.
,,	in sheepe	xj*li*.
,,	in swyne	vj*li*. xv*s*. viij*d*.
,,	in ducks and henns	xiiij*s*.
,,	in corn growinge upon land	lxxxx*li*. xiij*s*. iiij*d*.
,,	one lead sesteron	vj*li*. xiij*s*. iiij*d*.
,,	in fellies	xviij*s*. iiij*d*.
,,	in plowes	viij*s*.
,,	in tress carte ropps collors a cart sadle and other implements	xx*s*.
,,	a grindlstonn	ij*s*. vj*d*.
,,	carts waines and wheels	iiij*li*. x*s*.
,,	in racks	ij*s*. iiij*d*.
,,	in turves	xx*s*.
,,	sledds	ij*s*.
,,	in harrowes yoks axes nogers sawes siddropps an iron crowe and other implements	iij*li*.
,,	in bordes	x*d*.
,,	one tornell a stonnd and little peecs of wood	vj*s*.
,,	in spoks	v*s*.
,,	in malte	v*li*.
,,	in spades a hack and a showe	iij*s*.
,,	loss tymber swyne troughes and hewen stonns	vj*s*.
,,	in coles	vj*li*. xviij*s*. o
,,	litle peece of tymber	xij*d*.
,,	a table and formes in hall	xx*s*.
,,	in iron grats	iij*li*. xj*s*. iiij*d*.

43

Item	one still	iijs. iiijd.
„	three tables and a litle shelfe	xxs.
„	one cubbord	vjs. viijd.
„	a pare of virginalls	xxxs.
„	one payre of andirons	iijli. vjs. viijd.
„	twoe chires	iijs. iiijd.
„	one joynt chire	iiijs.
„	one other chire	vs.
„	a forme and three pickters	ijs. iiijd.
„	in racketts galborts a crowe a fyrepoote a pare of fire tongs and a shocoe	vs.
„	three greate chests	xls.
„	bordes formes and a settle	ixs. viijd.
„	a crab prise and a fiechbord	xijd.
„	in oatemeale	xxxs.
„	in flower	iijs. iiijd.
„	in grats barly and dust	iijs. iiijd.
„	in pewter	ixli. xs. vjd.
„	in broches a gridiorn and a pestle	vs.
„	twoe drippinge pannes	viijs. iiijd.
„	in pann brasse	xxxvjs.
„	in potte brasse	iijli.
„	an ould fryinge panne	iiijd.
„	an axe for a bucher two kynes a grater	xijd.
„	in haye	xijli.
„	in tringe vessels	iijli. xjs. vjd.
„	a throwe and twoe cheespress	vjs.
„	a saltinge lead and frame to it	xls.
„	in earthin potts	iis. vjd.
„	in bordes and a troughe	vjs. vjd.
„	a saffe	ijs. vjd.
„	a bord a form and shelves	ixs. ijd.
„	one ould cubbord	ijs.
„	frames to laye beare on with a troughe	iiijs.
„	brass coxe glass botles and a baskett	iiijs.
„	one chest	ijs. vjd.
„	twoe botles of woode	ijs.
„	one twil sheete and sacks	xxs.
„	one windle and twoe halfe metts	iiijs.
„	one whele swinglestock and a trapp	xd.
„	cheres and stowles	xviijd.
„	seffes and ridles	vjd.
„	noggins dyshes and trenchers	ijs.
„	in salte fleche	xxs.
„	in chesses	viijs.
„	in hopps and sope	xvjs. viijd.
„	in boxes a table and shelves	iijs.
„	in glasses	iijd.

Item	a case and trenchers	vj*d.*
,,	in woolen yorne and litle implements	viij*d.*
,,	in bedstocks	xj*li.* vj*s.* o
,,	one form and an ould chest	xij*d.*
,,	ould cradle and wiskett and a peec of a trunk	viij*d.*
,,	in matts	ij*s.*
,,	in beddinge	xxxvj*li.* vj*s.* viij*d.*
,,	one pillyon	ij*s.*
,,	in sadlcloathes	iiij*s.*
,,	one chest and a boxe within it	v*s.*
,,	in boxes shelves and a chire	iij*s.*
,,	one ould muskett barell	xij*d.*
,,	twoe tables	iiij*s.* iij*d.*
,,	in joynt stowles	ix*s.*
,,	in cheires and stowles	xxvij*s.* viij*d.*
,,	twoe ould carpetts	xviij*d.*
,,	in vallance curtains and rodds	v*li.* xvij*s.* viij*d.*
,,	one shelfe	viij*d.*
,,	one joynte press	xxvj*s.* viij*d.*
,,	one table and frame	ij*s.*
,,	one joynt cheire	vj*s.* viij*d.*
,,	in trunks and chests	iiij*li.* v*s.*
,,	one greene carpett	xxx*s.*
,,	greene velvett pillowes and quishons	v*li.*
,,	pillowes and quishons imbrothered	vij*li.* vj*s.* viij*d.*
,,	a cubbord cloath imbrothered	iij*li.* vj*s.* viij*d.*
,,	a bearinge cloath	xx*s.*
,,	a turkye carpett	xx*s.*
,,	fyve coveringes for quishons	x*s.*
,,	in lynnen	xxvij*li.* x*s.* v*d.*
,,	twoe tables more	ix*s.*
,,	one greene carpett	xij*d.*
,,	twoe cheires	vij*s.*
,,	one greene cubbord cloath	vij*s.*
,,	twoe ould carpetts mor	iij*s.* iiij*d.*
,,	in quishons	xxxvij*s.* viij*d.*
,,	one cipruswoode cheste	v*li.*
,,	one warming panne	ij*s.* vj*d.*
,,	one lookinge glass	ij*s.*
,,	one shelfe and skrines	xij*d.*
,,	in books	xviij*s.*
,,	in seellinge tymber	x*s.*
,,	in bordes and ashes	iij*s.*
,,	in a clocke and bell	xxvj*s.* viij*d.*
,,	two shelfes and a forme	xviij*d.*
,,	one lannthornn	x*d.*
,,	more in formes and borddes	ij*s.* vj*d.*
,,	one long ladder and pichforke	ij*s.*
,,	a pare of weighes for a gouldsmith	ij*s.*

Item another paire of weights		ij*s.*
,,	one bruche	vj*d.*
,,	tymber att More Mylne and Lower Mylne	v*li.* ij*s.*
,,	in flaxen cloath	xvj*s.*
,,	twoe saddles	iij*s.* iiij*d.*
,,	one gould ringe	l*s.*
,,	in plate	xviij*li.* ij*s.* iiij*d.*
,,	debts owinge unto the Testator at the tyme of his death	CClxxxxiij*li.*
,,	in money in the house	xx*li.* ix*s. ob.*
,,	in the deceaseds apparell	xij*li.*
	Exhibitum cum protestacione &c.	

866*li.* 12*s.* 10*d. ob.*[1]

[1] The inventory contains no formal Summa Totalis. This s$_\text{u}$·n and the two other arabic figures above were apparently added later.

THE ACCOUNTS
1667–78

Memorandum in the year beginning Michaelmas 1667 the mills toll was as followeth:

	Wheat		Barley		Meal		Malt	
	Windles	pecks	windles	pecks	windles	pecks	windles	pecks
Rylands mill	14	0	64	3	70	1 h.	24	2

which in money after the severall rates of corn in the afforsaid year amounts to 22*li*. 09*s*. 09*d*.

Moor mill	11	3 h.	67	2 h.	67	3 h.	19	1

which in money as afforesaid amounts to 19*li*. 12*s*. 01*d*.

An accompt of new corn housed at Michaelmas 1668 what the same yielded & how disposed of:

Oats	Threaves	Measures
In Upermost Legh	90 ⎫ which yielded	625
In Moor Hey	87 ⎭	
Barley		
In Morleg Meadow	69 ⎫	
In Legh on Back of Barn	48 ⎬ which yielded	259 h.
In Fearnhurst	33 ⎭	
Bean & Pease 5 acres	which yielded	183
Oats from Newton		093
Barley from Moor Mill		019 h.
Barley from Lower Mill		007 h.
Pease from Newton		004

The afforsaid corn was disposed of as followeth between Michaelmas afforsaid & Michaelmas 1669:

Oats	
To rideing horses and strangers horses	191
For work horses..	075 h.
For swine & pullen	178
Sold	103 h.
Made in meal	042
For seed	176
For doves	009
	675

Barley

For seed	042
Malted	160
For swine & pullen	060
Sold	006
For doves	007
For bread	009
For patridg	001
	285

Bean & pease

For rideing horses	015
For swine	013
Sold	110
For doves	006
For seed	025 h.
	169 h.

Toll gott in the year begining Michaelmas 1668

Lower Mill	Wheat windles	pecks	Barley windles	pecks	Meale windles	pecks	Malt windles	pecks
Xmas qutr.	5	2	17	2	23	0	6	0
Ladyday qutr.	3	1	17	0	36	2	8	0
Midsummer qutr.	2	1 h.	16	0	19	1 h.	5	2
Michaelmas qutr.	3	0	15	2	21	1 h.	10	0
per annum	14	0 h.	66	0	100	1	20	2

which in money after the severall rates of corn in the afforesaid year
amounts to: 28*li*. 1*s*. 0*d*.

Moor Mill	bushels	pecks	bushels	pecks	windles	pecks	bushels	pecks
Xmas qutr.	4	1 h.	26	3	27	0 h.	6	2
Ladyday qutr.	3	1 h.	17	1	23	0	5	2
Midsummer qutr.	1	1 h.	11	3 h.	9	2 h.	5	0
Michaelmas qutr.	0	3	6	1 h.	6	2	0	3
per annum	9	3 h.	62	1	66	1	17	3

which in money amounts to 20*li*. 15*s*. 11*d*.

An accompt of new corn housed at Michaelmas 1669 what the same yielded
and how disposed of:

Oats	Threaves	Measures
In Uppermost Legh	89 } which yielded	283
In Fearnhurst	21	
Memorandum: there was old oats at Michaelmas afforsaid about		30

Barley

In Legh on Back of Barn	155 } which yielded		265
Bean & pease 3 acres	which yielded		39
Oats from Newton	....		281

The afforesaid corn was disposed as followeth between Michaelmas afforesaid & Michaelmas 1670:

Oats

For swine & pullen	113 h.
For rideing horses & strangers horses.............................	198 h.
For work horses...	048
For doves	006
For seed	102
For fat beasts..	004 h.
totall	472 h.

Barley

Made in malt	183
For pullen	019 h.
For swine	003 h.
For seed	040
For bread	012 p.
For doves	003
totall	261 p.

Bean & pease

For swine	011
For doves	006 h.
For rideing horses	033 h.
totall	22 h.

Toll corn gott in the yeare begining Michaelmas 1669

Rylands Mill	*Wheat*		*Barley*		*Meal*		*Malt*	
	windles	pecks	windles	pecks	windles	pecks	windles	pecks
Xmas qutr.	5	0	25	2	34	3	5	0
Ladyday qutr.	1	1 h.	14	1	32	1	5	2
Midsummer qutr.	0	2	12	0	5	0	4	2
Michaelmas qutr.	2	1	12	2	17	1 h.	3	1
per annum	9	0 h.	64	1	89	1 h.	18	1

which in money comes to 29*li*. 3*s*. 11*d*.

Moor Mill	bushels	pecks	bushels	pecks	windles	pecks	bushels	pecks
Xmas qutr.	3	1 h.	26	3 h.	29	2 h.	5	0
Ladyday qutr.	2	1	16	3 h.	27	3	4	0
Midsummer qutr.	1	1 h.	8	2 h.	3	0 h.	2	2
Michaelmas qutr.	2	3	13	2	1	1	2	2
per annum	9	3	65	3 h.	61	3	14	0

which in money amounts 22*li.* 16*s.* 10*d.*

An accompt of new corn housed at Michaelmas 1670 what the same yielded and how disposed of:

Oats	Threaves		Measures
In Legh on Back of Barn	46	which yeilded	476
In Sussah Fields	50		
Bought 82 measures, from Newton 69 measures			151
		totall	627

Barley	Threaves		Measures
In Moor Hey	72		
In Legh on Back of Barn	30	which yeilded	178
Bought of Adam Hampson	32		
Bought			011
From Moor Mill			015
		totall	204
Memorandum: There was old bean about			016
Bought			037
		Totall	053

An accompt how the afforesaid corn was disposed of between Michaelmas afforesaid & Michaelmas 1671

Oats

For swine & pullen	099 h.
For rideing horses & strangers horses	136 h.
For work horses	045 h.
For fatt oxen	005 h.
For doves	014
For seed	108
Made in malt	126
Dried for swine	028
Sold after 1*s.* 3*d.* per measure	002
Total	565

Barley

Made in malt	120
For seed	027
For pullen	010 h.
For bread	014 h.
For swine	023 h.
For doves	004 p.
Totall	198 h.

Bean

For swine	018 p.
For rideing horses	001 h.
For seed	034
Totall	055 h.p.

Toll corn in the year begining Michaelmas 1670 was as followeth:

Rylands Mill	Wheat windles	pecks	Barley windles	pecks	Meal windles	pecks	Malt windles	pecks
Xmas qutr.	4	0	22	0	29	3	1	2
Ladyday qutr.	1	0	17	2	20	2 h.	4	0
Midsummer qutr.	1	2	19	0	11	1	3	2
Michaelmas qutr.	1	2 h.	17	1	12	2	2	2
per annum	8	0 h.	75	3	74	0 h.	11	2

which in money amounts to 33*li*. 2*s*. 2*d*.

Moor Mill	bushels	pecks	bushels	pecks	windles	pecks	bushels	pecks
Xmas qutr.	5	2	33	2	15	0 h.	2	3
Ladyday qutr.	1	3 h.	15	2	17	3	0	0
Midsummer qutr.	2	1	21	3 h.	08	0 h.	3	2
Michaelmas qutr.	1	0 h.	18	2	05	2 h.	3	0
per annum	10	3	89	1 h.	46	2 h.	9	1

In money 28*li*. 10*s*. 11*d*.

Memorandum: Hay-makeing in the year 1671
cost 8*li*. 3*s*. 1*d*.

An accompt of new corn housed at Michaelmas 1671 what the same yeilded & how disposed of:

	Threavs		Measures
Oats			
In Calf Hey	127	} which yielded	160
In Berry Ground	055		

Barley

In Sussay Fields	080 ⎫ which yielded		169
In Billinge upon 3 Roodland	014 ⎭		
Bought	044		
From Moor Mill	057 h.		

	Totall	270 h.
270 h.		

In Moor Hey containing about 4 acres) which yielded	061 h.
Bought	014 h.

	Totall	76

An accompt how the afforesaid corn was disposed of between Michaelmas afforesaid and Michaelmas 1672

Oats

To rideing horses & strangers horses	85 h.
For swine and pullen	88
For work horses	69
For doves	08
For coalts at Newton	12
Made in malt	82
Memorandum: there was about 4 measures of old malt	
For Mistris Legh's horse	09 h.
For seed	100

	Totall	454

Barley

Made in malt, besides about six measures of old malt	184
For swine	004
For pullen	030 h.
For making up batches at Rylands mill	021
For doves	006 h.
For seed	034

	Totall	270

Bean & pease

For swine	034 h.
For doves	008 h.
For the horses	004
For seed	013

	Totall	066

Toll corn gott in the year begining Michaelmas 1671 as followeth:

Rylands Mill	Wheat windles	pecks	Barley windles	pecks	Meal windles	pecks	Malt windles	pecks
Xmas qutr.	2	2 h.	18	1 h.	33	1 h.	3	2
Ladyday qutr.	1	0	20	2	33	2	3	2
Midsummer qutr.	2	1	14	3	21	3	3	0
Michaelmas qutr.	1	0	17	3	18	0 h.	8	0
per annum	6	3 h.	71	1 h.	106	3	18	0
In money	29.9.11.							

Moore Mill	bushels	pecks	bushels	pecks	windles	pecks	bushels	pecks
Xmas qutr.	3	0	29	2	28	3 h.	7	0
Ladyday qutr.	1	0	17	2	24	0	2	2
Midsummer qutr.	1	2	9	0	6	3	4	2
Michaelmas qutr.	2	0	13	2	3	0	2	2
per annum	7	2	59	2	62	2 h.	16	2
In money	22.6.1.							

Memorandum: Hay makeing in the year 72 cost about 5*li*.

Corn housed Michaelmas 1672 which yielded & was disposed of as followeth:

	Threavs	Measures
Barley		
In Calf Hey	100 } which yielded	312
In Moor Hey	038 }	
Bought		084
From Moor Mill		016 h.
From Rylands Mill		009
Totall		421 h.

	Threavs	Measures
Oats		
In Moor Hey	046 }	
In Lymed Piece	085 } which yielded	409
In Berry Ground	050 }	
From Newton		132
Bought		053
Totall		594

Pease which yielded   008 h.

The afforesaid corn was disposed of as followeth betwen Michaelmas afforsaid & Michaelmas 73

Oats

To rideing horses & strangers	118 h.
To swine & pullen	117
To draught horses	070
Made in malt	080
For fat oxen	003 h.
For seed	102
To Mistris Legh's horse	019
	570

Barley

Malted	264
For swine	038 h.
For pullen	028 h.
For bread	019
Seed	031 h.
For doves	020 h.
	402 h.

Bean

To swine	008

An accompt of the profits of the mills in the year begining Michaelmas 1672

Rylands Mill	Wheat windles	pecks	Barley windles	pecks	Meal windles	pecks	Malt windles	pecks
Xmas qutr.	4	2	20	1	31	3	5	1
Ladyday qutr.	3	3	21	0	23	0 h.	3	2
Midsummer qutr.	1	0	17	0	22	2	6	0
Michaelmas qutr.	4	0	20	0	07	2	5	2
per annum	13	1	78	1	84	3 h.	20	1
In money	22li. 7s. 10d.½							

Moor Mill	bushels	pecks	bushels	pecks	windles	pecks	bushels	pecks
Xmas qutr.	2	3	22	0	29	1 h.	5	0
Ladyday qutr.	1	1	21	0	38	1 h.	3	0
Midsummer qutr.	2	0	12	0	11	0 h.	3	0
Michaelmas qutr.	2	2	14	0	0	3	2	2
per annum	8	2	69	0	79	2 h.	13	2
In money	18.16.11.							

An accompt of what corn was housed in the harvest 1673, what the same yielded and what hath been received into garner, as also how the same hath been disposed of, as by the following accompts more particularly may appear, between Michaelmas 73 & 74

Barley	threavs	measures
In Calf Hey	71} which yielded	113 h.
Winstanley tith barley yielded		005 h.
Tith French wheat & barley		006 h.
From Moor Mill		027 h.
Newton Tith barley		094 h.
Newton tith French wheat & barley		002
	Totall	249 h.

Oats		
In Calf Hey	014⎫	
In marled ground	102 ⎬which yielded	405
In Lows	064⎭	
Winstanley tith oats for ⎱yielded my Master's part ⎰		186 h.
Old oats from Newton		092
Bought at 1s. 7d.		070
	Totall	753 h.
Bean & pease from Newton		3

Disposed off as followeth

Oats

To rideing horses & strangers	138
Swine & pullen (whereof 42 burnt)	225
Work horses	060
Mistris Legh's horse	027
Doves	019 h.
Malted	100
Seed	118
Sold..	004 h.
Made in meal	042
Totall	735

Barley

To swine & pullen	050
Malted	096
Bread	029
Sold..	004
Seed	050
Doves	009
Flower	004
	242
Bean & peas to swine	003

Memorandum: there hath been wheat spent }
this year, (none now remaining) }   040

Rye, (about 3 measures remaining in garner)   008

Barley malt spent about 60 for ale, & 110 for }
common beer (none now remaining) beside }   170
Eastern malt }

Oat malt spent about   080
beside about 20 being course was given
to horses & pullen.

[On a loose sheet]

An accompt what tithe corn hath come from Newton since Michaelmas 73.

	Rye	Wheat	Barley	Oats	Bean & pease	French wheat & barley
Dec.						
10		4			1 h.	2
16		4 h.				
20	0 h.		3		1 h.	
Jan.						
13			5			
Feb.						
2			5			
18			1 h.			
22			20			
28			4			
March						
9			4			
12			16			
18			16			
26			4			
Totall	0 h.	8 h.	94 h. & 10 sold	all sold	3	2

[On a loose sheet]

An accompt of what my Masters proportion (being the half) of Newton tith amounted to in the year 1674.

	Measures	li.	s.	d.
Oats sold at 2s. 2d. per measure	169	18	06	02
Brought home of the same rate	006	00	13	00
Sold at 1s. per measure	017	00	17	00
Used at Newton of 1s. per measure	007	00	07	00
Totall	199	20	03	02

	Measures	li.	s.	d.
Barley brought home at 4s. 2d. per measure	045	09	07	06
Brought home at 2s. per measure	002	00	04	00
Sold at 3s. 6d. per measure	010 h.	01	16	09
Sold of 3s.	015 h.	02	06	06
Light corn sold	014 h. for	01	05	00

	Measures	li.	s.	d.
Totall	87 h.	14	19	09

French wheat & barley sold at 3s. per measure	004 h.	00	13	06
Wheat brought home and to bring 5 h. which according as Samuel sold, comes to 1li. 15s. 4d.	005 h.	01	15	04
Wheat & rye to come home about	3 pecks at	00	03	00
Pease & bean to come home about	2 pecks	00	01	08

		li.	s.	d.
Totall vallue		37	16	5
Totall sold		25	14	11

	li.	s.	d.			
Of which received & paid my Master	18	0	00			
Paid for charges, as barnes, thresh- ing, winowing, carriage &c. besides the straw	00	14	00		22	6	6
To Samuel for 6 measures of barley	01	05	00			
More received now in mony	02	07	6			

And remaines to my Master owing by severall persons at Newton this 21 of June	02	18	5

An accompt of all oats received into garner since Michaelmas 73 when there remained of old oats about   12

	Bought oats	Old oats from Newton	Winstanley tithe	Demesne oats
September				
30			4 h.	
October 1				09
30		6		
November				
10		12	12	
18				16
28		12	42	
December 9		26		
10		18		55 h.
11		18		
February 7			32	14 h.
12				16 h.
21	70			

[continued on page 58

ERBFW—E

	Bought oats	Old oats from Newton	Winstanley tithe	Demesne oats
March	at 1s. 7d.			
12			11	06
29			52	49
Aprill				
18				43
June 20				43
July 15				96 h.
18				29
Totall	70	92	186	405

An accompt how the afforesaid oats have been disposed off since Michaelmas afforesaid

	Rideing horses & strangers	Swine & pullen	Work horses	Mistris Leghs horse	Doves	Malted	Seed	Sold	Made in meal
Oct.									
1	2	2				40 no			
10	2	1				old re-			
14	2	2				maining			
28	2	2		1					
Nov. 4	2	3		1					
11	3	3							
13	1 h.								
15	3	3		1					
22	3 h.	2		1					
29	3	3		1					
30	2	1 h.		1					
Dec. 5	3 h.	2							
13	5 strangers	42 burnt in drying		1	2				
20	3	4		1	2				
27	2 strangers	4		1					
Jan. 1	6 strangers	48 dryed	2		2				
3	3	2		1					
6	2	3	2		1 h.				
10	2 h.	4		1					
11	2 strangers				1 h.				
17	3	4	2	1	1				
24	3	3	2 h.	1	1 h.				
31	4	4 (3 strangers)	2 h.		1				
Feb. 7	3 h.	3	3	1	1 h.				
14	3	4	3	1	1				
21	3	3	3	1	1				
28	3	36 dryed	3	1	1				
Mar. 8	3	4	3	March 1 Mistris Legh accompted		40			

	Rideing horses & strangers	Swine & pullen	Work horses	Mistris Leghs horse	Doves	Malted	Seed	Sold	Made in meal
Mar. 14	4 h.	2	3	2	2 h.				
21	3 h.	3	4	1					
28			4	1					
Apr. 4	4	2	4	1		20	50 in Lows		
11	5	2	5	1					
18	3	1 h.	4	1				3 to James Ascroft	
29	4	2	4	1			68 in Calf		
May 8		2	4	2 Dr.			Hey	1 h. to Roger Penington	
12		2	2						
June 10		2							42
24		1 h.							
July 10		2							
16		2							
20	1	1							
Aug. 8	2	2							
13	12 h. for Mistris Legh	1							
24	2 h. Sir Richard Brook	1							
Sept. 4		1							
10	8 Sir John								
24	4 h.	2 h.							
Totall	138	225	60	27 all paid for	19 h.	100	118	4 h.	42

An accompt of what barley hath been received into garner since Michaelmas 73 when no old remained

	Newton tith barley & French wheat & barley	From Moor Mill	Tith French wheat & barley in Winstanley	Tith barley in Winstanley	Demesne barley
Oct.					
22		1 h.		3 h.	25
24		1 h.			
28		3 h.	4 h.		
Nov. 7		2	2	2	
Mar. 10		1 h.			
21	96	2 h.			
May 8					22 h.
23					45

[continued on page 60

	Newton tith barley & French wheat & barley	From Moor Mill	Tith French wheat & barley in Winstanley	Tith barley in Winstanley	Demesne barley
June 10					21
Aug. 15		3			
24		2 h.			
29		1 h.			
30		1 h.			
Sept. 9		1			
14		1 h.			
24		2			
28		2			
Totall	96	27 h.	6 h.	5 h.	113 h.

An accompt how the afforesaid barley hath been disposed off between Michaelmas 73 & 74

	Swine & pullen	Malted being old malt	Bread	Sold	Seed	Doves	Flower
Sept.		80					
30	2						
29	2						
Oct. 16	2						
27	1						
Nov. 6	2	32					
20	2						
27	1 h.						
Dec. 10	2						
18	2						
24	4						
Feb. 6	2 h.		o h.			1	
11	1 h.						1
17	1 h.		1			2 h.	
24	1		2			o h.	
Mar. 1.	1 h.		1			1	
4	2					1 h.	
21	1 h.	40	1 h.			o h.	
28	1 h.					1	
Apr. 1	2 h.						
10	o h.			1			
May 20	1	24	1 h.	1			
25	1		1 h.		50 h. in marled ground		
June							
2			3	2			
16			1 h.				
18			o h.				
24	1		1 h.				
30	1		1 h.				

	Swine & pullen	Malted being old malt	Bread	Sold	Seed	Doves	Flower
July 6	1						1
10			1 h.				
13	1						1
17	1		1				
21	1						
24	1		1				
29							1
Aug. 8	1 h.		2 h.				
17	1		1 h.				
24			2				
Sept. 2	1		1				
9	1		1 h.				
Totall	50	96	29	4	50	9	4

An accompt of the toll betwen Michaelmas 73 & 74

Rylands Mill	Wheat		Barley		Meal		Malt	
	windles	pecks	windles	pecks	windles	pecks	windles	pecks
Xmas qutr.	3	2	26	2	28	0 h.	3	0
Ladyday qutr.	2	1 h.	23	0	30	2	3	0
Midsummer qutr.	1	2	19	2	15	0	0	0
Michaelmas qutr.	0	2 h.	18	3	08	2	1	0
per annum	8	0	87	3	82	0 h.	7	0
In money	41li. 17s. 4d.							

Moor Mill	bushels	pecks	bushels	pecks	windles	pecks	bushels	pecks
Xmas qutr.	3	1 h.	20	1	24	3 h.	3	0
Ladyday qutr.	1	2	19	0	28	3 h.	0	0
Midsummer qutr.	1	2	18	0 h.	00	3	3	2
Michaelmas qutr.	3	1	21	1 h.	02	1	3	0
per annum	9	2 h.	78	3	56	3	9	2
In money	31li. 9s. 7d.							

Memorandum: in the harvest 1674 there was hay gott as followeth videlicet

	Loads	
In Rough Hey	15	
In Broad Meadow & Sussey Fields	17	the getting whereof cost 5 li. 14s. 1d.
In Moor Hey	16	
In Midle Legh	16	
Totall	64	

An accompt of what corn was housed in the harvest 1674 what the same yieldeth or otherwise hath been received into garner, as also how the same hath been disposed of between the 29 of September 74 & Michaelmas 75, as by the following accompts particularly may appear.

Oats	threavs		measures
In Lows	80 ⎫		
In Calf Hey	80 ⎬ which yielded		298
From Newton			006
Bought			018
		Totall	322

Barley			
In marled ground, videlicet,			
in Hardy Butts	80 ⎫		
in Pitterley	70 ⎬ which yielded		289
in Chadock Mead	72 ⎭		
From Moor Mill			059
From Newton tith			047
		Totall	395

The afforesaid corn was disposed of as followes between Michaelmas 74 & 75

Oats

To rideing horses and strangers	80
To swine & pullen	045
Pigeons	001
Drought horses	039
Colts	004 h.
Malted	023
Seed	120
Totall	312 h.

Barley

To swine & pullen	131 h.
For bread	049
Malted	142
Flower	001
Doves	008
Seed	048
Totall	379 h.

Memorandum: there hath been wheat ⎫ spent this year about ⎭	53 h.
And Rie	03
Malt for ale whereof 18 Derby malt	84
For comon beer barley malt	127
Oat malt	016 h.

As by the following particulars.

An accompt of all oats received into garner between Michaelmas 74 & Michaelmas 75, noe old ones remaineing.

	Demesne oats	Newton tith	Bought
November			
2	26 h.		
14	41		
17	47		
December			
24	24		
February 15	49 h.	6	
March 10	56		
Aprill 10	10 h.		
20	25		
May			
20	19		
July 1			3
August 14			3
30			12
	298	6	18

An accompt how the afforesaid oats have been disposed of between Michaelmas 74 & 75.

	Rideing horses & strangers	Swine & pullen	Pigeons	Drought horses	Colts	Malted	Seed
Nov.							
2	0 h.	1 h.					
5	1	1 h.					
8		1					
17	1	2					
18	6 dryed into 4	1					
25		2	1				
Dec.							
21	1	2					
25		1					
28	29 dryed	2					
Jan. 1	1	2					
9	2	2		2			
16	2	2		2			
23				2			
30				2			
February							
6				2			
13				2	1		
19		1					
20		1		2	1		
27	2 h.	1		2	1		
March							
3	2	1					50 in Lows
6				2			42 in Lower Salter 28 in
13	2	1		3			Har Salter
18	1	1 h.					

[continued on page 64

	Rideing horses & strangers	Swine & pullen	Pigeons	Drought horses	Colts	Malted	Seed
March							
20	2	1		3			
27	2 h.	1 h.		3			
Aprill 3	2			3 h.			
10	2	1 h.		3			
17	1	1 h.		3			
20					1 h.	23	
24	2			3			
28	1	1 h.					
May 20	7	2					
31	2	1					
June 1	1 h.	2					
9	1	2					
16	0 h.	1					
24		1					
30	1	1 h.					
July 3	6 h. to strangers	1					
Aug.							
30	6 h. to strangers						
	89	45	1	39	4 h.	23	120

An accompt of what barley hath been received into garnar since Michaelmas 74, when no old remained.

	Demesne barley	Moor mill barley	from Newton of tith
Oct.			
1		2 h.	
19		3	
24		1 h.	
29	40	2 h.	
Nov. 14	32	3 h.	
19	21	1 h.	
28		3	
Dec. 3	39		
5		3 h.	
12	20	2	
19	26 h.	3 h.	
January			
15		3	
23	16	2 h.	
30	00	2 h.	
Feb. 1	21		
24	39	2 h.	
March			
21	09	2 h.	
Aprill 3		2 h.	
10	14		

	Demesne barley	Moor mill barley	from Newton of tith
19		2 h.	
June 5	21		
	from Newton		47
July 10		3	
24		2	
Aug. 10		3	
17		2	
27		2	
Sept. 1		2 h.	
	289	59	47

An accompt how the afforesaid barley hath been disposed of between Michael-mas 74 and 75.

	To swine & pullen	Bread	Malted	Flower	Doves	Seed
Oct.						
9		1 h.				
23	2	1				
28	2	1	20			
Nov. 4	1	2 h.				
10	1 h.	0 h.		1		
14	2 h.		22			
17	2 h.	2				
19	2					
21	2					
23	2					
24	3 h. ground	1 h.			1	
27	2					
30	1 h.					
Dec. 1	1	2				
3	1 h.		40			
4	1 h.	1 h.				
7	3	3				
12	3	0				
17	3	2				
21	2 h.					
24	2					
27	2 h.					
30	2					
January						
1	2				1	
4	2 h.					
8	2					
9	3					
14	3	0 h.				
16	3				1	
18	3					
20	3					
22	3	0 h.			1 h.	

[continued on page 66

	To swine & pullen	Bread	Malted	Flower	Doves	Seed
Jan. 25	3					
30	3	2				
Feb. 3	3	2 h.			1 h.	
8	3					
11	3	3				
15	2 h.					
19	3	1 h.				
22	3	3	20		1	
24	3 h.					
27	2 h.					
March 2	3	1				
6	2				1	
9	2	3				
12	2 h.					
21	3	2 h.	40			
26	2					
Apr.						
1	2					
10	2 h.					
14	2	2 h.				
21	2	2 h.				
26	2					
May 6		1				48 in
June 1	2	0 h.				marled
6	2					ground
18	2					
24	2					
28	2	2 h.				
July 12	2	0 h.				
22	1 h.					
24	1					
Aug. 10	1 h.	1 h.				
	131 h.	49	142	1	8	48

An accompt what wheat & rye hathe been bought or otherwise received into garnar since Michaelmas 74.

The afforesaid wheat & rye hath been disposed as followth for house use.

	Memorandum: at Michaelmas there remained old about	wheat	rye			wheat	rye
		00	3				
Sept 24	From Newton	14		For seed	14		
Oct. 7	from Newton	06		Ground		1	0 h.
Nov. 4	from Newton	04		Oct. 17		1	
Dec.							
10	from Newton	04		28		0 h.	
				Nov.			

		wheat	rye
Dec. 17	Bought at 9s. 8d. per measure }	02	
Feb. 12	from Newton	03 h.	
27	from Newton	01	
Aprill			
May			
31	from Newton being tith corn }	04	
July			
1	Bought	2	
	from Newton being tith }	1 h.	
Aug.			
19	bought	2	
	More a present	2	
	Totall	49 h.	3

besides* from mills
about 5 or 6 measures

	wheat	rye
5	1	0 h.
12	1	
Dec. 2	1	0 h.
22	1 h.	
28	1	0 h.
January		
8		0 h.
9		0 h.
20	2	0 h.
Feb. 11	1	
22	1	
March 4	1	
17	1	
18	1	
22 for March beer		0 p.
Aprill		
1		0 h.
6		3 h.
22	2	
May		
20		1 h.
31	1	
June		
22	1	
July 8		1 h.
22		
Aug. 4		1 h.
12	1	
15		1 h.
26	1	
30	1	
Sept.		
4	2	
10	1	
20	1	
28		1 h.
Totall	53 3p.	2 h.

* 'what was' struck out.

An accompt what malt hath been made or otherwise received into garnar between Michaelmas 74 & 75 no old remaining

An accompt how the afforesaid malt hath been spent

		Barley malt	Oat malt
Oct			
17	Bought homs malt	06	
24	Bought homes malt	06	
29	Bought	06	
Nov.	Made 20 measures which being whet & course was but }	13	
10	Borrowed	12	
14	Made 22 measures which yielded }	18	
Dec.			
20	Made 40 measures which yielded }	39 h.	
Jan.			
16	Bought	06	
Feb.			
22	Made 20 which yielded (being bad) }	18 h.	
27	Bought	06	
	bought eastern malt }	12	
March			
16	bought	12	
22	bought Liverpool malt }	12	
	Made 40 which yielded }	40	
June	Bought eastern malt }	06	
22			
July			
1	Made 23 measures which yielded }		20
12	Bought homs malt }	06	
22	bought	6	
Aug.			
30	bought	6	
Sept.	Derby malt	6	
20	homs malt	6	
	Total made & received besides toll }	243	20
	Totall spent for ale 084, small beer 127, of barley; and 16 h. of oat. Pullen & geese 7 h. (viz.) }	219	16 h.

	Ale	Small beer Barly malt	Oat malt
Oct. 19		7	
29	6		
Nov.			
4	6		
10		10 being bad	
28		8	
Dec.			
7	7 h.		
10		8	
19		6 h.	
January			
8		9	
25	6		
Feb.			
8		9	
22	6		
March			
5		9	
16 for March beer }	12		
April			
7		8	
10	7		
May 1	0	9	
10	5		
30		09	
& for green geese 1			
June 1st for geese 1	5		
22		9	
July			
12	6		
14		5	5
22	6		
& for pullen 1			
30 for pullen 1			
Aug.			
3 for pullen 1			
5 for pullen 1			
6		5	5
& for pullen 1 h.			
12	5 h.		
21		5	5
30	6	4 h.	1 h.
Sept.			
20		6	

		geese	Ale	Small beer
Remains in garner		7 h.	084	127 16 h.
6 measures of				
Derby malt	*			
And the rest being				
very bad was taken				
for swine & pullen				
And about 5 measures				
oat malt for horses				

* 'To gees & pull:' struck out.

An accompt of how many threaves of tith were within the liberties of Newton in the year 1674 (Videlicet)

	threaves
Oats	190 ⎫
Barley	160 ⎪
Wheat	009 ⎬
French wheat	010* ⎪
Bean & pease	⎪
French wheat & barley	019 ⎭

* Whole entry struck out.

An accompt what hath arisen out of the afforesaid corn to my Master's proportion being the half.

		Oats	Barley	Wheat	Wheat & rye	French wheat & barley	Bean & pease
Feb.		measures	measures	measures	measures	measures	measures
27	brought home	6	2 light				
Apr.							
12	brought home		4				
16	brought home	7 used at Newton	8				
17	brought home		8				
19	home		4				
20	home		3				
21	home		9				
22	home		9				
May							
31				4	3 pecks home		2 pecks home
June	sold at 2s. 2d.	169	10 h.				
21	sold after 1s.	017	sold at 3s. 6d.			4 h. sold at 3s. per measure	
			15 h. sold at 3s.				
24	brought home		14 sold for 1s. 5d.	1 h.			
Totall of my Master's part is		199	086	5 h.	3 pecks	4 h.	2 pecks

An accompt of the mill profitts between Michaelmas 74 & 75

Rylands *Mill*	*Wheat* windles	pecks	*Barley* windles	pecks	*Meal* windles	pecks	*Malt* windles	pecks
Xmas qutr.	0	3	16	0	45	0	3	0
Ladyday qutr.	0	3 h.	15	0 h.	34	1 h.	0	0
Midsummer qutr.	0	0	21	3	04	1 h.	0	2
Michaelmas qutr.	2	0	25	0	16	1	3	3
Totall per annum	3	2	77	3 h.	100	0	7	1
Totall in money	52*li.* 14*s.* 5*d.*							

Moor Mill	bushels	pecks	bushels	pecks	bushels	pecks	bushels	pecks
Xmas. qutr.	3	0 h.	33	1	43	2	3	2
Ladyday qutr.	1	0	23	1	41	1	2	0
Midsummer qutr.	0	0	06	2	08	0	0	0
Michaelmas qutr.	2	0	18	2	13	2	1	2
Totall per annum	6	0 h.	81	2	106	1	7	1
Totall in mony								

Memorandum: in the harvest 75 there was hay gott as followeth, videlict

	Loads	
In Rough Hey	18	the getting
In Higher Moor Hey	11	whereof cost
In Middle Lee	30	5*li.* 17*s.* 2*d.*
In Lee on Back of Barn	28	
	115	

An accompt of what corn was housed in the harvest 75 and what the same yieldeth, as also what hath been received into garnar and how disposed of, as by the following accompt particularly appears.

	threavs	Measures
Oats		
In Lows	067	which yielded
In Salterleys	143	
Barley		
In marled ground	280 yielded	
Wheat		
In Bury ground	038	

An accompt of all oats winowed or otherwise received into garner between Michaelmas 75 & 76, no old remaining

	Demesne oats	from Newton
Oct.		
Sept. 1	08	
Nov. 4	07	
24	04	
30	45	
Dec. 4	30	
14	16	
January		
8	36	
Feb. 9	23	
March	6	
17	40	7
[18 or 19]	64	7 sold
25	63	
Aprill 1	61	
24	113	

An accompt how the afforesaid oats have been disposed off.

	Rideing horses & strangers measures	Swine & pullen measures	Draught horses measures	Mistris Leghs horse	Malted	for Mr. Peirs colt
Sept. 4	02					
8	01					
10	01	01				
16	01					
20	02	01				
Oct. 30 for stone colt	01					
Nov. 6		01		1		
12		01				
15	0 h.	01				
19	1	01				
22		01				
29	1 h.	01				
30		40 dryed for swine				
Dec. 4	2	01				
8	2	01			30	
13	0 h.	01				
16	1 h.					
20	1 h.					
23	1 h.		3			
27	1 h.					
30	2					
Jan. 8		2				
11	1	1	1 h.			
15	1					

[continued on page 72]

	Rideing horses & strangers measures	Swine & pullen measures	Draught horses measures	Mistris Leghs horse	Malted	for Mr. Peirs colt
Jan. 18	1 stra.					
22	1 stra.		3			
24	1 stra.	1				
29	2	1	3			
Feb. 5	3 ⎫ 1 stra. ⎭	1	3			
8	2					
10	2 stra.	1				
14	1	1 h.	3			
18	1	1				
19			3	Seed		
23	3	2		75 in		
26	1	1	3	Salterleys		
March 4	1 h.		3	45 in		
11	3		3	Sussa Fields		
18	3	1	4	29 in		7 sold &
25	3	1	4	Chadock medow	1	accompted
Aprill				34 in Bury Ground		for by
1	2	1	4		1	James
8	2	1	4		1	for 1s. 8d.
15	2 h.	1	4		1	
21	2	1	3	40	1	
29	2				1	
while I was at London						
Aug. 1		1 h.				
6		1				
10		2				

An accompt of what barley hath been winowed or received into garner since Michaelmas 75

	Demesne barley	Moor mill
Oct. 4	34 ⎫ threaves	
21	40 ⎬ 94	
25	48 ⎭	
Nov. 8	20	
24	34	2 h.
Dec. 4		2 h.
20		6
28	11	
Jan. 18	14	1 h.
24	13 h.	
March 4	45	3
May 1	52	

An accompt how the afforesaid barley hath been disposed off.

	Swine & pullen	Malted	Bread	Doves
Oct. 4	2	24		
10	2			
20	2	40		
29	1 h.	40		
Nov. 1	2			
4	2			
8	2			
12	2			
15	2		0 h.	
20	2 h.			
22	2			
25	3		2 h.	
30	3			
Dec. 4	3			
6	2			
9	2			
11	2		2 h.	
14	2 h.			
18	2			
20	2			
24	2			
January				
1	2			
4	2			
8	2			
11	2		1 h.	2
14	2			
17	2		1	2
22	2			1
24	2		0 h.	1
26	2			
31	1		1 h.	1 h.
Feb. 1	2			2
9	2			
12	2			1 h.
24	2		1	
26	1			1 h.
March				
4	1 h.	40		
11	1			
18	1 h.			
Apr. 1	1		2	
8	1			seed
May 1		41		14 in Hardy Butts

An accompt what wheat hath been winowed or received into garner since Michaelmas 75

	Demesn wheat
	measures
Aug. 18	13 h.
Feb. 22	04
May 1	01 h.
11	07
Aug. 1st	100

which was winowed whilst my Master was at London

An accompt how the said wheat hath been disposed off.

	For hall use	Seed	Sold
Aug. 20	1		
Sept. 30	1	seed	
Oct. 8	1	4 h.	
&	1 given Mistris Harrison		1 Peter
Nov. 5	1		
11	1		
14	1		
Dec. 20	0 h.		
January 11	1		
18	1		
Feb. 2	1		
10	0 h.		
22	1		
March 20	1		
Aprill 1	1		
8	1		
28	1		
May 1	1		
Aug. 1 by Peters accompt when my Master was at London			71 which as by accompt came to 13. 11. 8
Aug. 2	2		
& while at London as they tell me	4		
14	0 h.		
25	2		

An accompt of what malt hath been made or received into garner between Michaelmas 75 & 76

Sept.	Derby malt measures	Barley malt made measures	Oats malt made measures
29 rested in garner }	6		
Oct. 20		28	
Nov.			
9		42	
22		43	
Dec. 20	22		30
Feb. 2	11		
Apr. 8		43 h.	
18			
May			
15			44
Totall	039	156	74

An accompt how the same malt hath been disposed of.

Oct.	Ale measures	Small beer barley malt measures	oat malt measures	measures
20	6	8		12 which
Nov.				was
9		8		owing
29	6	8		to
Dec.				Garswood
14		8		
Jan.				
20	6	5	5	
Feb.				
6		6	4	
28		4	6	
March				
4	6			
8	12 for March beer			
30		4	6	
Aprill				
18		4	6	
21	5			1 given Peter
whilst at London				
May				
18		5	5	
June				
12		5	5	
July				
25	6			1 for geese
Aug.				
10		5	5	
Oct. 4		5	5	
Totall	47	75	47	14

Malt made & received
into garnar this year   measures
videlicet
    Derby malt   039
    Homes malt   156
    Oat malt   074
                       ——

Totall spent between
Michaelmas 75 & 76
    For ale & March beer   047 ⎞
    For small beer of ⎞   075 ⎠
    barley malt   ⎠
    & of oat malt   047
    Owing to Garswood ⎞
    & given   ⎠   014
                       ——
    Soe remaines in ⎞
    Derby malt &   ⎬   059
    homes malt   ⎠
    In oat malt   027

An accompt of threavs of tith in Newton in the year 1675

                                 threaves
        Oats   250 ⎞
        Barley   100 ⎟
        Wheat   012 ⎟
        Rye   002 ⎬
        French [wheat] & barley   004 ⎟
        Bean   003 ⎟
        Pease   004 ⎠

An accompt of the mill profits in the year begining Michelmas 1675

Rylands Mill	Wheat		Barley		Meal		Malt	
	windles	pecks	windles	pecks	windles	pecks	windles	pecks
Xmas qutr.	3	2	16	2	38	0 h.	0	0
Ladyday qutr.	2	1 h.	11	0	19	3 h.	2	0
Midsummer qutr.	0	3	04	1	15	3	3	2
Michaelmas qutr.	2	2	03	2	12	2	2	2
Totall per annum	9	0 h.	35	1	86	1	8	0
Totall in money								
Moor Mill								
Xmas qutr.	3	2	18	2	50	1	0	0
Ladyday qutr.	0	2	12	2	30	0	2	0
Midsummer qutr.	1	1	00	0	24	3	0	0
Michaelmas qutr.	3	0	07	0	13	2	3	2
Totall per annum	8	1	38	0	118	2	5	2
Totall value								

An accompt of what corn was housed in the harvest 1676 what the same yielded
and how disposed off between Michaelmas 76 & 77

threavs

Wheat	011 yielded
Barley in Hardibutts	yield
Oats	
In Salterleys	120
in Chaddock meadow	060
Bury Ground	060
Sussay Fields	074
Pease & bean	018 h.

An accompt of all oats winowed and received into garnar between Michaelmas
76 & 77, no old ones remaining

Measures

Oct.	
2	06
12	67
Nov. 16	07
24	55
Dec.	48
Jan. 25	94
Feb. 16	65
17	44
March 12	35
Apr. 12	31
May 3	64
July 9	106
Sept. 20	040

An accompt how the said oats have been disposed off.

Oct.	Swine & pullen	Rideing	Mr Peirs horse	Mistris Leghs	Malted	Draught horses
2	1	2				
6	1	0 h.	1			
14	1 h.	1	1			
17	1					
20	1					
21	1	0 h.	1			
27	41 dried					
28	1 h.	1	1			
28	1					
30	1					
Nov. 1	1 h.	1				
4	1 h.	1 h.	1			
9	1 h.					
11	0	1 h.	1			
16	1					
18	1	1 h.	1			
21	1					

[continued on page 78

	Swine & pullen	Rideing horse	Mr Peirs horse	Mistris Leghs	Malted	Draught horses
Nov. 24	2	1 h.	1			
28	1 h.					
Dec. 2	1 h.	2				
5	1 h.					
8	1 h.	0 h.				
9	0	1 h.				
12	1 h.					
16	1 h.	1	1	1		
23	2	1 h.	1	1 accompted		
30	2	1 h.	1	1		
Jan. 6	1	1 h.	1	1		
8					40	
13	2	1 h.	1	1		
	6 h. dryed for swine					
20	2	1 h.	1	1		
25	2					
27	1	1	1	1		
Feb. 3	1 h.	1	1	1	3	
10	2 h.	1	1	1	3	
15	2					
16	2					
17	1 h.	1	1	1	3	
22	3 dryd					Pigeons
24	1 h.	1	1	1	3	1 h.
27	1 h.					1 h.
March 3	1 h.	1 h.	1	1	3	1 h.
7	1					
10	1	1	1	1	3	0 h.
14	1					1 h.
17	1 h.	1	1	1	3	
24	1	1	1	1	3	1 h.
31	1	1 h.	1	1	3	
Apr. 7	1	1 h.	1	1	3	
13	1	1 h.	1	1	Seed 3	
20	2 h.				74 Salterlays	
27	1	1	1	1	3	
May 3	1 h.	1	1	1 June 11	33 Chadock meadow	
10	1 h.			Mistris Legh	13 Pitterley	
14	1			went abroade	21 Medow Moor Hey	
20	1			Returned Sept. 3		
July 2 whilst I was at London					Malted 24 18 made in meal	

Swine & pullen	Rideing horse	Mr Peirs horse	Mistris Leghs	Malted	Draught horses
			Sept. 17 Mistris Legh accompted		
			1		
Sept. 22			1		
29			1		

An accompt of all barley winowed and received into garnar since Michaelmas 76 no old remaining.

	measures	Bought
Sept. 30	51	
Nov. 11	21	
May 1		7

An accompt how the said barley hath been disposed off.

	Swine & pullen	Malted	Bread
Sept. 30	1 h.	40	
Oct. 3	2		
10	1 h.		
16	1 h.		
20	1		
24	1		
30	1		
Nov.			
1	0 h.		
4	0 h.		
11	2		
18	1		
21	1		
28	1 h.		
Dec. 1	1		
5	0 h.		
8	1		
12	0 h.		
16	1		
20	1 h.		
26	1		
Jan. 18	0 h.	0 h.	
20	1		
25		1 h.	
Feb. 3	1		
9	0 h.		
14	0 h.		
16	1		

[continued on page 80

	Swine & pullen	Malted	Bread
March 9			1

Pease & bean received
Winowed

Nov.	
1	1 h.
3	17

Pease & bean delivered
Swine

Nov.		
1	0 h.	
9	0 h.	
16	1	
18	0 h.	
21	0 h.	
24	0 h.	
25	02	
28	10	
Dec. 1	0 h.	
7	0 h.	
12	1	
Jan. 25	0 h.	6 malted
Feb. 3	1	
10	1	
16	1	

An accompt what wheat hath been received into garnar since Michaelmas 76

	Measures 4 old Winowed
Dec.	
4	6
Jan. 8	4
13	22
& course sort }	03
Sept. 6	08 bought for seed
13	03 bought seed

An accompt how the afforesaid wheat hath been disposed off.

	house use
Oct.	
2	1
6	1
24	1
Dec. 1	1
15	1
Jan.	
20	1
Feb.	
10	1
20	1
March	
2	1
8	1
24	1
Apr. 3	1
15	1
28	1
May 6	1
15	1
25	1
June 1	1

	house use
June. 24	1
at severall times to Michaelmas 77	9
	28

Sept.
12 for seed   10 measures

An accompt what malt hath been made or received into garnar since Michaelmas 76	An accompt how the same malt has been disposed off.

Measures			
	Derby malt	homes malt	Oat malt
Sept. 29 Rested in garner old malt	7 old	49 old	20 old
Oct. 20		47	
Feb. 3			42
March 24	6		24 May 10,
Sept. 17		00*	
18		06 bought	

Oct.	Ale measures	Small beer		
		Barley malt	oat malt	
16	6			
24		5	5	1 given
Nov. 16		5	5	Peter
Dec. 1	6			
8		6	4	
Jan. 9		5	5	
30	6			
Feb. 5		5	5	
March 2		5	5	
24	12 for March beer			
Apr. 1	06			
20	06			0 h.
May 1		5	5	
20	06			
June 10		5	5	
24	06			
July 10		4	6	
Sept. 12		4	6	

* '30 bought' entered in error by accountant, 'bought' struck out & '3' overwritten 'o'

Memorandum: hay making in the year 78 cost 5*li*. 1–10 two Meadow Leghs & Broad Meadow being only good.
Corn housed Michaelmas 1677

	threaves
Barley	027
Oats	
In Salterleys	117
Chaddock medow	057
Petterley	026
Medow Moor Hey 2 acre	040

The afforesaid barley winowed since Michaelmas 77

	Winowed measures
Oct.	
27	45
Dec. 1	00*

* '77' overwritten 'oo'

Disposed of the said barley as follows

	Swine & pullen measures	Malted measures
Oct. 27	01	40
Nov. 10	01	
18	01	
Dec. 6	01 h.	
	04 ½	40

Oats winowed & received into garnar since Michaelmas 77

Sept. 29	Remained old oats
Oct. 27	45 new
Dec. 1	77 old
Jan. 2	64 old
28	114 old
	020 new
Feb. 27	072 new
March 16	018
29	050
July 1	86

Disposed of the said oats as followes

	Swine & pullen	Rideing horses	Mistris Leghs horse	Malted	Work horses
Sept.					
29	01 h.				
Oct. 6	02	03	01		
13	40 dryd	03	01		
20	03	03	01		
27	01	03	01		
Nov. 3	02	03	01		
10	02	03	01		
17	02	03	01		
24	02	03	01		
Dec. 1	02	03	01		
8	02	03	01		
15	02	04	01		
22	03	03	01		
29	02	03	01		

	Swine & pullen	Rideing horses	Mistris Leghs horse	Malted	Work horses
January					
5	01 h.	03	01		
12	02	03	01		
19	03	04	01		
26	02	04	01		
28				20	
Feb. 2	02	05	01		02
9	01	04	01		02
16	02	04	01		02
23	01	04	01		02
March					
2	01	04	01		03
9	01	05	01		03
16	01	04	01		03
			hitherto (viz) 17th March Mistris Legh setled all accompts		
23	02	04			
30	01	04	02		05
Aprill					
6	02	04	01	30	03
13	01	04	01		03
20	01 h.	03	01		03
27	02	01	01		03
May 4	01	01			
10	02	01	01		
29	03		01		
June 1	02	01	01		
10	02	01	0		
16	02	0			
20	02	01			
July 6	03	01			
13	02	03			
15	02	03	01		
27	02	04			
Aug. 6	02	03			
13	01	03			
20		04			
Sept. 1	02	03			
8	01	04			
17	01	03			
22	00	04			
29	02	04			

Memorandum: September 17th Mistris Legh evened all accompts with my Mistris for horse &c.

Malt received into garnar since Sept. 29

Disposed of the said malt as follows

77

Sept.	Barley malt	Oat malt
29 old	00	20
30 bought	30	
Oct. 10 bought	30	
25	42 made	
March 20	06 measures bought at Orrell which was given by Mistris Legh	
May 23		30

	Ale	Small beer Barley	Oat
Oct.			
6		04	06
10	6		
27		04	06
Nov. 19	6		
Dec. 8		05	05
Jan. 13		05	05
Feb. 5		05	05
March			
4		05	05
14	6		
30	12		
Apr.			
7		5	5
May 5		5	5
29		5	5
June 28	5	5	5
July 10	5		
20		5	5
Aug. 20		5	5
Sept. 5	6		
20		5	5

Wheat received Michaelmas 77

Disposed of as follows measures

Sept. 29 old

	measures
Sept. 29	01
Oct. 10	01
22	01
Nov. 12	01
24	01
Dec. 10	01

Corn housed Michaelmas 1678

	threaves
Wheat In Hardibuts	33
Barley In Meadow Moor Hey 2 acres	60
Oats	
In Brick Salterley	
Pitterley	
Chadock Meadow	

Oats received into garner since Michaelmas 78

	old	new
Oct. 1	70	
Nov. 9	24	
22	18 h.	
Dec.		
3	28	
27	06 h. new	
31	09 new	
Jan. 4	40 new	
17	23 new	
Feb. 4	56 h. new	
5	60 new	
March 6	53 new	
17	21 old	
Apr. 5	18 old	
	36	
May 23	72	
June 18	57	
	591 h.	

Disposed of the said oats as follows

To	Swine & pullen	Rideing horses	Mistris Leghs horse	Malte	Draught horses	Doves	Seed
Oct. 1	38 dryd			22			
7	02	02	01				
14	01	03					
24	01	02	01				
Nov. 1	02	04	00				
18	03 dryd		01				
19	02						
22	03	03					
30	03	03	01				
Dec.							
4	03 dryd	01 h.					
	02						
7	02	02	01				
10	01 h.	01 h.					
14	01 h.	03	01				
21		03	01				
25	02	01					
27		03	01				
31	02	02					
Jan. 3	02	02	01				
17	02		01				
	42 dryd for swine & part made into meal for poor						
25	02	02	01				

To	Swine & pullen	Rideing horses	Mistris Leghs horse	Malte	Draught horses	Doves	Seed
Feb. 1	02	02	01				
4	02 01 h.				1 h.	01	
10	02	03	01		2 0	01 h.	
17	02	03	01		2 0	01	
26	02	03	01		2	01	
March							
1	03	03	01		3	01	
8	03	03	01	24	3		
15	03	03	01				

Memorandum: March 17th Mistris Legh evened all accompts for board & horse to this day after 11*d.* measure & 18*d.* a week for hay & grasse

To	Swine & pullen	Rideing horses	Mistris Leghs horse	Malte	Draught horses	Doves	Seed
22	02	03	01		3		
29	02	03	01		3		28
Apr. 5	01	03	01		3		Chadock
7	02	2	1		3		Medow
14	01	2	1		3		25
21	02	3	1	0	3		Pitterley
30	01	2	1		3		42 Moor
			1				Hey Hier
May 23				20			
	110	76	26	66	34	05 h.	95
30	002	03					
June 5	001						
10	002	01					
19	001 h.	03					
26	003	01					
July 10	004	02					
20	005	01					
Aug. 10	004	01					
Sept. 1	003						
10	004						

050 for strangers, videlicet Sir Richard & Mr Legh

    139 h.

Barley received into garnar since Michaelmas   78

Disposed of as follows

	Winowd		Malted	Swine & pullen	Bread
Oct.		Oct.			
1	44	1	40		
Nov. 22	27	10		2	
Dec. 24	03 p. from mill	Nov. 22	23	1 h.	
May 1	44	29		1 h.	
		Dec. 2		1	
		8		1	
		15		0 h.	
		Jan.			
		16			01

Winowd		Malted	Swine & pullen	Bread
May				
May				
7		19	Seed	
			12 in Meadow Moor Hey	
			13 in Hardbuts	

Wheat received as follows, no old remaineing		Disposed of as follows		
			house use	seed
Oct. 1	17	Oct. 1		13
Dec.		2	01	
3	13 h.	20	01	
24	01 p. from mill	Nov. 1	01	
May 12	07 h.	10	01	
		Dec. 3	01	
		20		1 h.
		Jan. 5	00 h.	to
		18	01	Mistris
		29	01	Harrison
		Feb. 6	01	
		12	01	
		20	01	
		March		
		10	01	
		20	01	
			10 p. for March beer	
		27	01	
		Aprill		
		5	01	
		15	01	
		29	01	
		May		
		Aug.		
		1		8 sold
				1 sold
				1 sold
				4 sold

Malt received into garnar since Michaelmas 78			Disposed of as follows			
	Barley malt	Oat malt		Ale	Small beer Barley	Oat
		10 old remaining at Michaelmas	Oct.			
Oct. 22	44		22	06		
Nov. 20	11 from Mistris Legh		26		5	5
Dec.		23½	Nov. 11		5	5
21	25		30	07		

[continued on page 88]

	Barley malt	Oat malt			Ale	Small beer Barley	Oat	
March			Dec.					
30		24	8			5	5	
Apr.			16			5	5	
3	18 bought of Thomas Atherton at 13s. per load		24			0		1 to Peter
May			Jan.					
20	22 more of Thomas at same rate		20			5	5	
20	20 malted		27		06			1 to
June			Feb. 4					Mistris
15		24	March					Legh
Aug.			1			5	5	
13	06 Mistris Bispham		17		12 for March beer		0½ for	
	Totall 146	81½	Aprill				March	
			1			6	5	
			6			5	5	
			May					
			6			5	5	
			13		03			
			20					1 to
			June					Peter
			11			5	5	
			16		5			
			July					
			10			5	5	
			16		5			
			31			2½	2½	
			Aug					
			5			2½	2½	
Sept. 29			14			2½	2½	
Spent	056 for ale		19			2½	2½	
	076 small beer		30		6			
Total	132		Sept. 1			5	5	
		075½ small beer	22			5	5	
			26		6			
					56	76	75½	3

An accompt of the profitt of Rylands Mill for the year begin January 1st 78

	Wheat		Barley		Meal		Malt	
January	windles	pecks	windles	pecks	windles	pecks	windles	pecks
11	0	0						
18								
25								

[The following rentals are entered in the reverse of the same book]

THE RENTALS
1668(?)–77

	Christmas Rent		Midsummer Rent	
	s.	d.	s.	d.
Peter Ascroft	07	00	06	00
Widow Cowley de Billinge	01	00	01	00
William Bolton	03	04	03	04
James Bolton	01	08	01	08
Winstandley's on Moor	08	01	05	01
Lawrence Farclough	15	09	13	09
Richard Wareing	01	02	01	02
Raph Green	01	08	01	08
Pemberton house	00	03	00	03
Peter Rainford	03	06	02	06
George Winstanley	01	02	01	02
Henry Winstanley quaker	05	00	05	00
Thomas Atherton	02	06	02	06
Raph Widowson	03	00	02	00
Thomas Winstanley	02	00	01	06
John Taylor	02	06	02	00
Thomas Fairhurst	02	06	02	06
George Bibbie	17	09	14	09
Ewton Eaton de Billing	00	01	00	00
Lawrence Marsh	01	00	00	06
Henry Winstanley	11	00	08	00
Window Cartwright	02	00	01	06
Allice Bibbie	02	00	01	00
Allice Winstanley	03	09	03	09
Thomas Taylor	01	09	01	06

	Christmas Rent			Midsummer Rent		
John Winstanley	0	01	02	0	01	02
Henry Winstanley quaker	0	05	00	0	05	00
Thomas Atherton	0	02	06	0	02	06
Raph Widowson	0	02	00	0	03	00
Thomas Winstanley	0	02	00	0	01	00
Thomas Fairhurst	0	02	06	0	02	06
John Taylor	0	02	06	0	02	00
George Bibbie	0	17	09	0	14	09
Ewton Eaton, Billinge	0	00	00	0	00	01
Lawrence Marsh	0	01	00	0	00	06
Henry Winstanley	0	11	00	0	08	00
Widow Cartwright	0	02	00	0	01	06
Allice Bibbie	0	02	00	0	01	00
Allice Winstanley	0	03	09	0	03	09
Thomas Taylor	0	01	09	0	01	06
John Wood	0	13	04	0	13	04
	totall 20—12—13			totall 16—3—9		

A Rentall for Billinge Winstanley & Orrell made in the year 1669	Midsummer Rents			Boon capons hens & geese	Xmas Rent boon capons hens & gees added[1]			Plowing	Harrowing	Shearing	Mucking
Gilbert Barton	1	00	08	two fatt geese	1	03	8	one acre	one acre	one acre	one day leading
Widow Maddock	0	15	10	two hens & two capons	0	18	10	half an acre	half an acre	half an acre	1 day leading
Widow Cowley	0	05	05	two capons two hens	0	08	05			one day shearing	one day heaving
George Rainford	0	09	02	two fatt capons	0	12	02		one day	two days	two fillers
Henry Orrell	0	06	08	two capons	0	08	08	one day		two days	one day leading
Roger Penington	0	06	08	two capons one hen	0	09	02	half an acre:	or half acre	two days	1 day leading
								or in liew of mucking plowing or harrowing 4s. at Midsummer			
Winstanley's de Hill	0	07	01	two fatt capons two hens	0	11	00	one day	two days	two days	one day leading
Margaret Orrell	0	10	07	two fatt capons	0	13	07	one day		two days	1 day leading
Robert Whetherby	0	05	00	three hens	0	06	06			two days	
Robert Winstanley alias Sundeforth	0	19	08	three capons three hens	1	04	03	three rood land	three rood land	three rood land	one day leading
Richard Farclough	0	04	11	two fatt capons	0	07	11			one day	one day heaving
Richard Orrell	0	15	00	two capons two hens	0	18	00	one day	one day	two days	one day leading
Thomas Rothwell	0	02	00	one henn	0	02	06			one day	one day heaving
William Wareing	0	01	00	one henn	0	01	06				

[1] 'being added' in continuing headings.

A Rentall for Billinge Winstanley & Orrell made in the year 1669	Midsummer Rents			Boon capons hens & geese	Xmas Rent boon capons hens & gees added[1]			Plowing	Harrowing	Shearing	Mucking
Alexander Rylands	o	03	10	2 capons	o	05	09			one day	one day leading
Robert Atherton	o	03	06	2 capons	o	05	06			one day	one day heaving
Peter Lyon	o	05	02	two capons two hens	o	08	02	one day		two days	
Raph Taylor	o	01	08		o	01	08				
Widow Cowchett	o	01	06	four hens	o	03	06			2 days	one day heaving
Adam Hampson	o	03	02		o	04	00			one day	one day heaving
Thomas Chadwick	o	06	06	two capons two hens[3]	o	09	06	one day[2]		two days	one day heaving
James Green	o	01	03	one capon	o	02	03			one day	one day heaving
William Cartwright	o	01	09	3 hens	o	03	04				
John Woods	o	13	04		o	13	04	one day		3 days	one day leading
Richard Orrell	o	01	03	one	o	01	08			one day	one day heaving
Thomas Rylands	o	04	00	one fatt capon	o	05	06			one day	one day heaving
Richard Penington	o	02	00		o	02	00				
Mathew Fairhurst	o	02	00		o	02	00				
Robert Rainford	o	03	04	3 hens	o	04	10			two days	one day hooking
Omfrey Atherton	o	02	04	one capon	o	03	04			two days	one day heaving
William Chadwick	o	00	11	one capon one hen	o	02	05			one day	one day heaving
Henry Cowley	o	01	09		o	02	00				one day heaving
Oliver Withington	o	08	04	two capons two hens	o	11	04	one day		3 days	one day leading
William Barton	o	06	02	two capons two hens	o	09	02	one day		two days	1 day leading

[1] 'being added' in continuing headings.
[2] 'remitted in the new lease' substituted later.
[3] 'remitted in the new lease, being deminished' substituted later.

A Rentall for Billinge Winstanley & Orrell made in the year 1669	Midsummer Rents	Boon capons hens & geese	Xmas Rent boon capons hens & gees added[1]	Plowing	Harrowing	Shearing	Mucking
Nicholas Atherton[2]	0 02 03[3]	two capons two hens	0 05 03[4]	one day		two days	1 day leading
Oliver Hasledean	0 00 06	one hen	0 01 00			two days	
Edward Strickland	0 01 00	one hen	0 01 06			one day	1 day filling
Robert Winstanley alias Dennis	0 01 10	one capon one hen	0 03 03			one day	1 day heaving
William Eaton	0 05 00	two hens	0 06 00			two days	1 day heaving
Jane Penington	0 00 03	one hen	0 00 09				
Edmund Atherton	0 01 10	one capon	0 02 10			one day	one day heaving
Lawrence Derbishire	0 13 10	two capons two hens	0 16 00	half an acre		half an acre	1 day leading
James Ascroft	0 02 00		0 02 00			two days	one day heaving
Peter Ascroft	0 06 00	two hens	0 07 00			one day	one day heaving
Widow Cowley de Billinge	0 01 00		0 01 00			two days	
William Bolton no counterpart[5]	0 03 04		0 03 04			two days	
James Bolton no counterpart[5]	0 01 08		0 01 08			half an acre	
Hugh Heskett	0 05 01	two capons two hens	0 08 01			two days	1 day heaving
Lawrence Farclough	0 13 09	two capons	0 15 09	half an acre		half an acre	1 day leading
Richard Wareing	0 01 02		0 01 02			one day	1 day heaving
Raph Green	0 02 06	one fatt capon	0 04 00				
Pemberton house	0 00 03		0 00 03				
Peter Rainford	00 03 08	one capon	0 04 08			one day	one day heaving
John Winstanley	00 01 02		0 01 02			one day	one day heaving
Henry Winstanley quaker	00 05 00		0 05 00				
Thomas Atherton	00 02 06		0 02 06				

[1] 'being added' in continuing headings.
[2] Substituted for 'Gaskel's house'.
[3] '0 03 06' struck out.
[4] '0 06 06' struck out.
[5] Added later.

A Rentall for Billinge Winstanley & Orrell made in the year 1669	Midsummer Rents			Boon capons hens & geese	Xmas Rent boon capons hens & gees added[1]			Plowing	Harrowing	Shearing	Mucking
Raph Widowson	00	03	00	one capon	0	04	00			one day	one day heaving
Thomas Winstanley	00	01	06	one hen	0	02	00			one day	one day heaving
Thomas Fairhurst	00	02	06		0	02	06				
John Taylor	00	02	00	one hen	0	02	06			one day	
George Bibbie	00	14	09	two capons two hens	0	17	09			two days	one day leading
Ewan Eaton de Billinge	00	00	00		0	00	01				
Lawrence Marsh	00	00	06		0	01	00			one day	one day heaving
Henry Winstanley	00	08	00	two capons two hens	0	11	00	one day = or in lieu of all boons 6s. 8d.		two days	one day leading
Widow Cartwright	0	01	06	one hen	0	02	00			one day	
Allice Bibbie	0	01	00	two hens	0	02	00			one day	
Peter Marsh[2]	0	0	3		0	0	3			one day	one day heaving

Totall tenants 67
in Billinge
Winstanley &
Orrell

	capons		hens	days	&	acre	days	&	acre	days	&	acres	carts
Total yearly boons	52	&	60	10	&	3¾	4	&	2¾	78	&	3¾	17
More													
John Southworth	0	2	6	0	0	2	6			one day	one day & all the rest of tenants heave being about 49		

1 'being added' in continuing headings.   2 This item added later.

A Rentall for Billinge Winstanley and Orrell made Christmas 1670	Christmas Rent			Midsummer Rent		
	li.	s.	d.	li.	s.	d.
Gilbert Barton	1	03	08	1	00	08
Widow Maddock	0	18	10	0	15	10
Widow Cowley	0	08	05	0	05	05

A Rentall for Billinge Winstanley and Orrell made Christmas 1670	Christmas Rent			Midsummer Rent		
	li.	s.	d.	li.	s.	d.
George Rainford	0	12	02	0	09	02
Henry Orrell	0	08	08	0	06	08
Roger Penington	0	09	02	0	10	08
Winstanley's de Hill	0	11	00	0	07	01
Thomas Jameson	0	13	07	0	10	07
Robert Weatherby	0	06	06	0	05	00
Robert Winstanley alias Sundforth	1	04	03	0	19	08
Richard Farclough	0	07	11	0	09	11
Richard Orrell	0	18	00	0	15	00
Thomas Rothwell	0	02	06	0	02	00
William Wareing	0	01	06	0	01	00
Alexander Rylands	0	05	09	0	03	10
Robert Atherton	0	05	06	0	03	06
Peter Lyon	0	08	02	0	05	02
Raph Taylor	0	01	08	0	01	08
Widow Cowchett	0	03	06	0	01	06
Adam Hampson	0	04	00	0	03	00
Thomas Chaddock	0	09	06	0	06	06
James Green	0	02	03	0	01	03
William Cartwright	0	03	04	0	01	09
Richard Orrell	0	01	05	0	01	06
Thomas Rylands	0	05	06	0	04	06
Richard Penington	0	02	00	0	02	00
Mathew Fairhurst	0	02	00	0	02	00
Robert Rainford	0	04	10	0	03	04
Omphrey Atherton	0	03	04	0	02	04
William Chaddock	0	02	05	0	00	11
Henry Cowley	0	02	00	0	01	09
Oliver Withington	0	11	04	0	08	04
William Barton	0	09	02	0	06	02
Gaskell's house	0	06	06	0	03	06
Oliver Hasledean	0	01	00	0	00	06
Edward Strickland	0	01	06	0	01	00
Robert Winstanley alias Dennis	0	03	03	0	01	10
William Eaton	0	06	00	0	05	00
Jane Penington	0	00	09	0	00	03
Edmund Atherton	0	02	10	0	00	10
James Ascroft	0	02	00	0	02	00
Lawrence Derbishire	0	16	00	0	13	00
Peter Ascroft	0	07	00	0	06	00
	15	00	08	11	09	01
Widow Cowley de Billinge	0	01	00	0	01	00
William Bolton	0	03	04	0	03	04
James Bolton	0	01	08	0	01	08
Hugh Heskett	0	08	01	0	05	01
Lawrence Farclough	0	15	09	0	13	09
Richard Wareing	0	01	02	0	01	02

A Rentall for Billinge Winstanley and Orrell made Christmas 1670	Christmas Rent			Midsummer Rent		
Raph Green	0	04	00	0	02	06
Pemberton house	0	00	03	0	00	03
Peter Rainford	0	03	06	0	02	06
John Winstanley, Boller	0	01	02	0	01	02
Henry Winstanley, Quaker	0	05	00	0	05	00
Thomas Atherton	0	02	06	0	02	06
Raph Widowson	0	04	00	0	03	00
Thomas Winstanley	0	02	00	0	01	06
Thomas Fairhurst	0	02	06	0	02	06
John Taylor	0	02	06	0	02	00
George Bibbie	0	17	09	0	14	09
Ewan Eaton de Billinge	0	00	00	0	00	01
Lawrence Marsh	0	01	00	0	00	06
Henry Winstanley	0	11	00	0	08	00
Widow Cartwright	0	02	00	0	01	06
Allice Bibby	0	02	00	0	01	00
Allice Winstanley	0	03	09	0	03	09
Thomas Taylor	0	01	09	0	01	06
John Wood	0	13	04	0	13	04
	5	11	0	4	13	04
Totall	20	11	08	16	02	05
				16	02	05

A Rentall for Billinge Winstanley and Orrell made Christmas 1671	Christmas Rent			Midsummer Rent		
	li.	s.	d.	li.	s.	d.
Gilbert Barton	1	03	08	1	00	08
James Maddock	0	18	10	0	15	10
Widow Cowley	0	08	05	0	05	05
George Rainford	0	12	02	0	09	02
Henry Orrell	0	08	08	0	06	08
Roger Penington	0	09	02	0	10	08
Winstanley de Hill	0	11	00	0	07	01
Mr Jameson	0	13	07	0	10	07
Robert Whetherby	0	06	06	0	05	00
Robert Winstanley alias Sundforth	1	04	03	0	19	08
Richard Farclough	0	07	10 ob.	0	04	11
Richard Orrell	0	18	00	0	15	00
Thomas Rothwell	0	02	06	0	02	00
William Wareing	0	01	06	0	01	00
Alexander Rylands	0	05	09	0	03	10
Robert Atherton	0	05	06	0	03	06
Peter Lyon	0	08	02	0	05	02
Raph Taylor	0	01	08	0	01	08
Widow Cowchett	0	03	06	0	01	06

A Rentall for Billinge Winstanley and Orrell made Christmas 1671	Christmas Rent			Midsummer Rent		
Adam Hampson ⎤	o	04	00	o	03	00
hereafter ⎦	o	04	00	o	03	02
Thomas Chaddock	o	09	06	o	06	06
James Green	o	02	03	o	01	03
William Cartwright	o	03	04	o	01	09
Richard Orrell, vide ⎤ Thomas Taylor ⎦	o	o	o	o	o	o
Thomas Rylands	o	05	06	o	04	00
Richard Penington	o	02	00	o	02	00
Mathew Fairhurst	o	02	00	o	02	00
Robert Rainford	o	04	10	o	03	04
Humphrey Atherton	o	03	04	o	02	04
William Chaddock	o	02	05	o	00	11
Henry Cowley	o	02	00	o	01	09
Oliver Withinton	o	11	04	o	08	04
William Barton	o	09	02	o	06	02
Nicholas Atherton ⎤	o	06	06	o	03	06
hereafter ⎦	o	04	00	o	03	06
Oliver Hasledean	o	01	00	o	00	06
Edward Strickland	o	01	06	o	01	00
Robert Winstanley alias Dennis	o	03	03	o	01	10
William Eaton	o	06	00	o	05	00
Jane Penington	o	00	09	o	00	03
Edmund Atherton	o	02	11	o	01	10
James Ascroft	o	02	00	o	02	00
Lawrence Derbishire	o	16	00	o	13	00
Peter Ascroft	o	07	00	o	06	00
Widow Cowley de Billinge	o	01	00	o	01	00
William Bolton	o	03	04	o	03	04
James Bolton	o	01	08	o	01	08
John Hesketh	o	08	01	o	05	01
Lawrence Farclough	o	15	09	o	13	09
Richard Wareing	o	01	02	o	01	02
Raph Green	o	04	00	o	02	06
Pemberton house	o	00	03	o	00	03
Peter Rainford &[2] for ⎤	o	03	06[1]	o	02	06[1]
Hampson's Croft hereafter[2] ⎦	o	04	08[2]	o	03	00[2]
John Winstanley boller	o	01	02	o	01	02
Henry Winstanley quaker	o	05	00	o	05	00
Thomas Atherton	o	02	06	o	02	06
Raph Widowson	o	04	00	o	03	00
Thomas Winstanley	o	02	00	o	01	06
Thomas Fairhurst	o	02	06	o	02	06
John Taylor	o	02	06	o	02	00
George Bibby	o	17	09	o	14	09
Ewan Eaton de Billinge	o	00	00	o	00	01

[1] Struck and crossed out.
[2] Interlineated later: '& for Hampson's ... o 03 00'.

A Rentall for Billinge Winstanley and Orrell made Christmas 1671	Christmas Rent	Midsummer Rent
Lawrence Marsh	0 01 00	0 00 06
Henry Winstanley	0 11 00	0 08 00
Widow Cartwright	0 02 00	0 01 06
Allice Bibby	0 02 00	0 01 00
Thomas Taylor	0 03 02	0 03 00
John Wood	0 13 04	0 13 04
James Orrell	0 03 09	0 03 09

{ hereafter 1:6: is to be deducted, for a parcell of ground my Master bought of Thomas Turner—videlicet

	0 03 00	0 03 00

A Rentall for Billinge Winstanley & Orrell made Jan. 1st 1672	Xmas Rent 1672	Mid-summer rent 73	Xmas Rent 73	Mid-summer 74	Christ-mas 74	Mid-summer 75
	li. s. d.	li. s. d.				
Gilbert Barton	1 03 08	1 00 08	1 3 8	01 00 8	1 3 8	1 0 8
James Maddock	0 18 10	0 15 10	0 18 10	00 15 10	00 18 10	0 15 10
Widow Cowley de Dam	0 08 05	0 05 05	0 08 05	00 05 05	00 08 05	0 05 05
George Rainford	0 12 02	0 09 02	0 12 02	00 09 02	0 12 02	00 09 02
Henry Orrell	0 08 08	0 06 08	0 8 8	00 06 08	00 08 08	00 6 8
Roger Penington	0 09 02	0 10 08	0 9 2	00 10 08	00 09 02	0 10 08
Winstanley de Hill	0 11 00	0 07 01	0 11 00	00 07 01	00 11 00	0 7 1
Mr Jameson	0 13 07	0 10 07	0 13 07	00 10 07	00 13 07	0 7 07
Robert Wetherby	0 06 06	0 05 00	0 06 06	00 05 00	00 06 06	00 05 00
Robert Winstanley alias Sundforth	1 04 03	0 19 08	1 04 03	00 19 08	01 04 03	00 19 08
Richard Farclough	0 07 10½	0 04 11	0 07 10½	00 04 11	00 07 10	0 4 11
Richard Orrell	0 18 00	0 15 00	0 18 0	00 15 00	00 18 00	0 15 00
Thomas Rothwell	0 02 06	0 02 00	0 02 06	00 02 00	00 02 06	0 2 0
William Wareing	0 01 06	0 01 00	0 01 06	00 01 00	00 01 06	0 01 00
Allexander Rylands	0 05 09	0 03 10	0 05 09	00 03 10	00 05 09	00 03 10
Robert Atherton	0 05 06	0 03 06	0 05 06	00 03 06	00 05 06	00 03 06
Peter Lyon	0 08 02	0 05 02	0 08 02	00 05 02	00 08 02	0 5 2
Raph Taylor } James Peningtons } Usher[1]	0 01 08	0 01 08	0 01 08	00 01 08	00 01 08	00 01 8
Widow Cowchett	0 03 06	0 01 06	0 03 06	00 01 06	00 03 06	0 01 6
Adam Hampson	0 04 00	0 03 02	0 04 00	00 03 02	00 04 00	0 03 2
Thomas Chaddock	0 09 06	0 06 06	0 09 06	00 06 06	{ 0 0 0 being remitted the widow[1]	00 6 6
James Green	0 02 03	0 01 03	0 02 03	00 01 03	00 02 03	00 1 3
William Cartwright } Edmund Atherton[1] }	0 03 04	0 01 09	0 03 04	00 01 09	00 03 04	0 1 9

[1] Added later.

A Rentall for Billinge Winstanley & Orrell made Jan. 1st 1672	Xmas Rent 1672	Mid-summer rent 73	Xmas Rent 73	Mid-summer 74	Christ-mas 74	Mid-summer 75
Thomas Rylands	0 05 06	0 04 00	0 05 06	00 04 00	00 05 06	0 4 0
Richard Penington	0 02 00	0 02 00	00 02 00	00 02 00	00 02 00	0 02 00
Mathew Fairhurst	0 02 00	0 02 00	00 02 00	00 02 00	00 02 00	0 2 00
Robert Rainford	0 04 10	0 03 04	0 04 10	00 03 04	00 04 10	0 3 4
Humphrey Atherton	0 03 04	0 02 04	0 03 04	00 02 04	00 03 04	0 2 4
William Chaddock	0 02 04	0 01 00	0 02 4	00 01 00	00 02 04	0 1 0
Henry Cowley	0 02 00	0 01 09	0 02 00	00 01 09	00 02 00	0 1 9
Oliver Withington	0 11 04	0 08 04	00 11 04	0 08 04	00 11 04	0 8 4
William Barton	0 09 02	0 06 02	0 9 2	0 06 02	00 09 02	0 06 02
Nicholas Atherton	0 04 00	0 03 06	0 4 0	00 03 06	00 04 00	0 03 06
Oliver Hasledean	0 01 00	0 00 06	0 1 0	00 00 06	00 01 00	0 00 6
Edward Strickland	0 01 06	0 01 00	0 01 06	00 01 00	00 01 06	0 01 0
Robert Winstanley Dennis	0 03 03	0 01 10	0 3 3	00 01 10	00 03 03	0 1 10
William Eaton	0 06 00	0 05 00	0 06 00	00 05 00	00 06 00	0 5 00
Jane Penington	0 00 09	0 00 03	0 00 09	remitted	remitted	remitted
Edmund Atherton	0 02 10	0 01 10	0 02 10	00 01 10	00 02 10	0 1 10
James Ascroft	0 02 00	0 02 00	0 02 00	00 02 00	00 02 00	0 2 0
Lawrence Derbishire	0 16 00	0 13 00	0 16 00	00 13 00	00 16 00	0 13 00
John Mosse	0 07 00	0 06 00	0 07 00	00 06 00	00 07 00	0 6 00
Widow Cowley de Billinge	0 01 00	0 01 00	0 01 00	00 01 00	00 01 00	0 1 0 hereafter Thomas Atherton
William Bolton	0 03 04	0 03 04	0 03 04	00 03 04	00 03 04	0 3 4
Totall	15 1 00½	11 12 2	15 1 0½	11 12 2		
James Bolton	0 01 08	0 01 08	0 01 08	0 01 08	00 01 08	0 1 8
John Hesket	0 08 01	0 05 01	0 8 1	0 05 01	00 08 01	00 05 01
Lawrence Farclough	0 15 09	0 13 09	0 15 09	0 13 09	00 15 09	00 13 09
Richard Wareing	0 01 02	0 01 02	0 01 02	0 01 02	00 01 02	0 01 02
Raph Green	0 04 00	0 02 06	0 04 00	0 02 06	00 04 00	0 02 06
Pemberton house	0 00 03	0 00 03	0 00 03	0 00 03	00 00 03	0 00 03
Peter Rainford	0 04 08	0 03 08	0 04 08	0 03 08	00 04 08	0 03 08
John Winstanley Boller	0 01 02	0 01 02	0 01 02	00 01 02	00 01 02	00 01 02
Henry Winstanley Quaker	0 05 00	0 05 00	0 05 00	00 05 00	00 05 00	0 5 0
Thomas Atherton	0 02 06	0 02 06	0 02 06	00 02 06	00 02 06	0 02 06
Raph Widowson	0 04 00	0 03 00	0 4 0	00 03 00	00 04 00	0 03 00
Thomas Winstanley	0 02 00	0 01 06	0 02 00	00 01 06	00 02 00	0 1 6
Thomas Fairhurst	0 02 06	0 02 06	0 02 06	00 02 06	00 02 06	0 2 6
John Taylor	0 02 06	0 02 00	0 02 06	0 02 00	00 02 06	0 2 0
George Bibby	0 17 09	0 14 09	0 17 09	00 14 09	00 17 09	0 14 9
Ewan Eaton de Billinge	0 00 00	0 00 01	0 00 00	00 00 1	00 00 00	0 0 1
Lawrence Marsh	0 01 00	0 00 06	0 01 00	00 00 06		
Henry Winstanley	0 11 00	0 08 00	Remitted for losse by Delf			
Widow Cartwright	0 02 00	0 01 06	Remitted being poor			

A Rentall for Billinge Winstanley & Orrell made Jan. 1st 1672	Xmas Rent 1672	Mid-summer rent 73	Xmas Rent 73	Mid-summer 74	Christ-mas 74	Mid-summer 75
Allice Bibby	0 02 00	0 01 00	Remitted being poor			
Thomas Taylor	0 03 02	0 03 00	0 03 02	00 03 00	00 03 02	
John Woods	0 13 04	0 13 04	0 13 04	00 13 04	00 13 04	0 13 04
James Orrell	0 03 00	0 03 00	0 03 00	00 03 00	00 03 00	0 03 00
Peter Marsh	00 00 00	00 00 00	0 00 0	00 00 03		
			James Rainford		0 02 00	0 02 00
	5 8 6	4 10 11				
	15 1 0	11 12 2				
Total Xmas Rent	20 9 6½	16 3 1				
Henry Winstanley, Anne Cartwright & Allice Bibby being remitted the whole is	19 14 6½					
Totall Midsummer rent the same being remitted is	15 2 7					

A Rent Roll made Jan. 1st 1675	Xmas Rent *l. s. d.*	Midsummer Rent 76 *li. s. d.*	Xmas 1676 *li. s. d.*		
Gilbert Barton	1 3 8	1 0 8	1 3 8	1 0 8	1 3 8
James Maddock	0 18 10	0 15 10	0 18 10	0 15 10	0 18 10
Widow Cowley de Dam	0 8 5	0 5 5	0 8 5	0 5 5	0 8 5
George Rainford	0 12 2	0 9 2	0 12 2	0 9 2	0 12 2
Henry Orrell	0 8 8	0 6 8	0 8 8	0 6 8	0 8 8
Roger Penington	0 9 2	0 10 8	0 9 2	0 10 8	0 9 2
Winstanley's de Hill	0 11 0	0 7 1	0 11 0	0 7 1	0 11 0
Mr Jameson	0 13 7	0 10 7	0 13 7	0 10 7	0 13 7
Widow Wetherby	0 6 6	0 5 0	0 6 4	0 4 10	0 6 4
			4d. being charged on Thomas Birchall		
Robert Winstanley	1 4 3	0 19 8	1 4 3	0 19 8	1 4 3
Robert Winstanley for Dennis house	0 3 3	0 1 10	0 3 3	0 1 10	0 3 3
Richard Farclough	0 7 10½	0 4 11	0 7 10	0 4 11	0 7 10
Richard Orrell	0 18 0	0 15 0	0 18 0	0 15 0	0 18 0
Thomas Rothwell & another[1]	0 2 6	0 2 0	0 2 6	0 2 0	0 2 6
William Wareing	0 01 6	0 1 0	0 1 6	0 1 0	0 1 6
Alexander Rylands	0 05 9	0 3 10	0 5 9	0 3 10	0 5 9
Robert Atherton	0 05 6	0 3 6	0 5 6	0 3 6	0 5 6
Peter Lyon	0 08 2	0 5 2	0 8 2	0 5 2	0 8 2
James Penington Usher for Raph Taylors	0 01 8	0 1 8	0 1 8	0 1 8	0 1 8
Widow Cowchett	0 03 6	0 1 6	0 3 6	0 1 6	0 3 6

A Rent Roll made Jan. 1st 1675	Xmas Rent (l. s. d.)	Midsummer Rent 76 (li. s. d.)	Xmas 1676 (li. s. d.)		
Adam Hampson	0 4 0	0 3 2	0 4 3	0 3 5	0 4 3
& Pemberton house[1]	0 0 3[1]	0 0 3[1]			
Humphrey Chaddock	0 9 6	0 6 6	0 8 0 memorandum		0 8 0
hereafter by			Receipt with Peter		
equall portions			for 6s.[2] 0 8 0		
James Green	0 2 3	0 1 3[3]			
Edmund Atherton for⎱ Cartwright's house ⎰	0 3 4	0 1 9	0 3 4	0 1 9	0 3 4
Thomas Rylands	0 5 6	0 4 0	0 5 6	0 4 0	0 5 6
James Penington Usher	0 2 0	0 2 0	0 2 0	0 2 0	0 2 0
Mathew Fairhurst	0 2 0	0 2 0	0 2 0	0 2 0	0 2 0
Robert Rainford	0 4 10	0 3 4	0 4 10	0 3 4	0 4 10
Humphrey Atherton	0 3 4	0 2 4	0 3 4	0 2 4	0 3 4
William Chadock	0 2 4	0 1 0	0 2 4	0 1 0	0 2 4
Henry Cowley	0 2 0	0 1 9	0 2 0	0 1 9	0 2 0
Oliver Withington	0 11 4	0 8 4	0 11 4	0 8 4	0 11 4
William Barton	0 9 2	0 6 2	0 9 2	0 6 2	0 9 2
Nicholas Atherton	0 4 0	0 3 6	0 4 0	0 3 6	0 4 10
Oliver Hasledean	0 1 0	0 0 6	0 1 0	0 0 6	0 1 0
	13 0 9½	9 17 11			
Edward Strickland	0 1 6	0 1 0	0 1 6	0 1 0	0 1 6
Henry Heaton	0 6 0	0 5 0	0 6 0	0 5 0	0 6 0
Jane Penington	0 0 9	0 0 3	0 0 9	0 0 3	0 0 9
Edmund Atherton	0 2 10	0 1 10	0 2 10	0 1 10	0 2 10
James Ascroft	0 2 0	0 2 0	0 2 0	0 2 0	0 2 0
Widow Derbishire	0 16 0	0 13 0	0 16 0	0 13 0	0 16 0
John Mosse	0 7 0	0 6 0	0 7 0	0 6 0	0 7 0
Thomas Atherton &	0 2 6	0 2 6	0 2 6	0 2 6	0 2 6
for Smith Cowley's	0 1 0	0 1 0	0 1 0	0 1 0	0 1 0 not paid
William Bolton	0 3 4	0 3 4	0 3 4	0 3 4	0 3 4
James Bolton	0 1 8	0 1 8	0 1 8	0 1 8	0 1 8
John Hesketh	0 8 1	0 5 1	0 8 1	0 5 1	0 8 1
Richard Farclough	0 15 9	0 13 9	0 15 9	0 13 9	0 15 9
Richard Wareing	0 1 2	0 1 2	0 1 2	0 1 2	0 1 2
Raph Green	0 4 0	0 2 6 ⎱			
and for James house[2]	0 2 3[2]	0 1 3[2] ⎰ 0 6 3	0 3 9	0 6 3	
Pemberton house[3]	0 0 3[3]	0 0 3[3]			
Peter Rainford	0 4 8	0 3 8	0 4 8	0 3 8	0 4 8
John Winstanle de Moor Mill	0 1 2	0 1 2	0 1 2	0 1 2	0 1 2
Henry Winstanley Quaker	0 5 0	0 5 0	0 5 0	0 5 0	0 5 0
Raph Widowson	0 4 0	0 3 0	0 4 0	0 3 0	0 4 0
Thomas Winstanley	0 2 0	0 1 6	0 2 0	0 1 6	0 2 0
Thomas Fairhurst	0 2 6	0 2 6	0 2 6	0 2 6	0 2 6
John Taylor	0 2 6	0 2 6	0 2 6	0 2 6	0 2 6
George Bibby	0 17 9	0 14 9	0 17 9	0 14 9	0 17 9

[1] Inserted later.   [2] Crossed out later.   [3] Whole entry cancelled.

A Rent Roll
made Jan. 1st 1675

	Xmas Rent			Midsummer Rent 76			Xmas 1676		
	l.	s.	d.	li.	s.	d.	li.	s.	d.
Ewan Eaton	0	0	0	0	0	1	0	0	0	0	0	1

Ewan Eaton	0 0 0	0 0 1	0 0 0	0 0 1
Henry Winstanley Remitted for losse by delf				
Ann Cartwright Remitted being poor				
Allice Bibby Remitted being poor				
Lawrence Marsh	0 1 0	0 0 6	0 1 0	0 0 6	0 1 0
Thomas Taylor	0 3 2	0 3 0	0 3 2	0 3 0	0 3
John Woods	0 13 4	0 13 4	0 13 4	0 13 4	0 13 4
James Orrell	0 3 0	0 3 0	0 3 0	0 3 0	0 3 0
Peter Marsh	0 0 3	0 0 3	0 0 3	0 0 3	0 0 3
James Rainford	0 2 0	0 2 0	0 2 0	0 2 0	0 2 0
John Southworth for the Riddiards 5s.[1]	– – –	– – –	– – –	0 2 6	0 2 6
Thomas Rothwell for Mosse Heys	0 1 6	0 1 6	0 1 6	0 1 6	0 1 6
Robert Wareing for Span Heys	0 0 0	0 1 6	0 1 6	0 1 6	0 1 6
John Corles for part of Wetherby's tenement 5s.[1]				
Thomas Wright for Span Hey Wood 1s.				
Thomas Birchall for a croft of Wetherbies & for glad in Croft Brook & Limd Bottom 1s. and for Widow Wetherbys crof 4d.				

          6 17   5   6   0   1

[1] '5s.' added later.

INDEX PERSONARUM

INDEX LOCORUM

(Field and similar names are shown in italics)

INDEX RERUM

(Glossarial)